HILLS I'LL PROBABLY LIE DOWN ON

Other Books by Rachel

Essay
Parenthood: Has Anyone Seen My Sanity?
The Life-Changing Madness of Tidying Up After Children
This Life With Boys
We Count it All Joy

Poetry
This is How You Know
Life: a definition of terms
The Book of Uncommon Hours

To see all the books Rachel has written, please click or visit the link below:
www.racheltoalson.com/writing

Rachel Toalson

HILLS
I'LL PROBABLY
LIE DOWN ON

BATLEE PRESS

Batlee Press
PO Box 591596
San Antonio, TX 78259

Copyright ©2018 by Rachel Toalson
All rights reserved.

No part of this book may be reproduced or transmitted in any form or by any means, electronic or mechanical, including photocopying and recording, or by any information storage and retrieval system, without permission in writing. For information, address Batlee Press, PO Box 591596, San Antonio, TX 78259.

The author appreciates your taking the time to read her work. Please consider leaving a review wherever you bought it, or telling your friends how much you enjoyed it. Both of those help spread the word, which is incredibly important for authors. Thank you for your support.
www.racheltoalson.com
www.crashtestparents.com

Manufactured in the United States of America

First Edition—2018/Cover designed by Toalson Marketing
www.toalsonmarketing.com

*To J.M.T., who taught me to choose my battles.
So glad you're here.*

Contents

Accept, Don't Regret
5

I'm Too Tired to Fight
65

Things that Make You Throw Up Your Hands
103

What It Looks Like on Top of the Hill
151

Hills that are Hardly Hills
193

Hills I'm Not Willing to Lie Down On
255

Foreword

When I first became a parent, I entertained elaborate ideas about how wonderful a parent I would be: my children would never throw tantrums, would never argue about anything, would never, ever, absolutely never say they hated me or wished they had a different mom—because, of course, I would be a reasonable parent with no unrealistic expectations of my children.

In other words, I was a perfect parent until I became a parent.

My first son charged into the world with a strong will, a sticky brain, and the kind of persistence that never backs down. He was just like me.

We fought on so many hills. In one day, we could fight about what shoes he was going to wear, whether he needed socks as a barrier between bare foot and tennis shoe, what food was available for lunch, how much time we had left at the park, whether or not we could actually fly (he remained convinced that we could; I remain convinced that he will solve this technicality when he is grown), and whether or not one should take a moment to tie a shoe.

As time went on, my son honed his stamina and his logic,

and those hills started looking more like mountains with tall, pointy, intimidating peaks. We'd wrestle and push and pull, both of us determined, both of us unmoving, both of us so exhausted by the end of it that I, for one, could hardly slide back down the peak on my backside.

I know that's frightfully vague—but the battles have merged in my mind and become a very large pile of regret. Eventually, I figured out it was better to pick my battles and pick them well.

I'd heard the wisdom, over and over again, in different circles—from pastors, from Husband, from my very wise mother. I probably should have just listened—but my son got his stubbornness from somewhere. You're welcome, Husband.

So I started choosing my battles. I started fighting for the things that were important—his identity, his view of the world, his heart—and left the not-so-important things—what he wanted to wear, what he preferred to eat, how many nights he could wear his oversized onesie to bed—on their populous hills.

This book is a celebration of children, a laughter-filled look at all their quirks and idiosyncrasies and contradictions (and my own, too, as a parent), a surrender flag every parent must decide for himself or herself to yield. These are the hills I'll probably lie down on—because there are much more important hills I'd rather die on for the sake of my sanity, my sons' well being, and a joyful family life together.

These essays are not arranged chronologically; they are collected into chapters that make the most sense—which means that in one essay a kid might be four years old, followed by one in which he is five, followed by another in which he is magically four again. No, I have not solved the secret to turning back time; I simply arranged the essays in the most logical form I could. I must ask for your tolerance here; my children, it seems, are always having birthdays, and those birthdays are not always logically placed within the timeline of Mama's humor essay ideas.

I hope you find joy, mirth, and courage in these pages as we traverse the hills of parenthood—enough to say, at the very least: *I have lived and I have loved, and that is enough.*

ACCEPT, DON'T REGRET

Things You'll Give Up When You Become a Parent

There are many things you don't ever think about before you become a parent—things no one will find it necessary to mention to you, either (even though there are many things they *will* mention to you unnecessarily).

I read so many books before I became a parent, but I was still ill-prepared for all the things I would have to give up.

You give up so much. You give up things like:

Long phone calls.

Every time I start to dial the number of a doctor or someone I need to talk to (because I hardly ever call the people I actually *want* to talk to), it doesn't take my children long to realize what's happening. In fact, I usually have to tell the hold music to hold on—because one of my twins has taken out the rake from his daddy's shed and is running toward the other twin with said rake raised above his head and a guttural yell straight from the pages of *Lord of the Flies* tripping along ahead of him. It's always my luck that the hold music stops and a person actually answers the phone when I'm in mid-yell—"Cut it out, or you'll have to come sit with me for the duration of this call!" I don't apologize. Instead, I usually pretend they didn't hear anything.

They probably didn't. Their "How can I help you?" didn't sound worried at all. It was my imagination.

Real dates.

If you have as many kids as I have, a date can seem like a luxury. Husband and I haven't had a real date in four months—and by real date, I mean a date that actually gets you out of the house. It's not because there are no babysitters willing to sit on a Friday night and watch my kids sleep but because we'd have no money left, after paying a sitter (or two), to actually have a date. I suppose we could ride around in the car looking at Christmas lights (for a three-week span during the year) or walk through a park (the temperate climate of South Texas is limited to the same three-week span; who wants to sweat on a date or freeze half to death?) or recline the van seats and take a long, uninterrupted nap.

But I'd like, for once, to have a restaurant-cooked dinner where kids weren't hanging around outside the door, peering through the crack between the bottom of the door and the floor, whispering that they'd like to have some French fries once in a while, too. A dinner out would be nice now and then.

Extended conversations.

We try really hard to teach our children not to interrupt, unless there's an emergency. The problem is that kids have a very hard time defining "emergency." They will interrupt us to tell us the computer froze while they were playing Minecraft (this was unauthorized play, an observation that will come with a whole half hour of argument). They'll interrupt us to ask why rain tastes like dirt mixed with sky mixed with musty fart (they're the kids of a poet; what do you expect?). They'll interrupt us to tell us all about the cut they just got on their finger—the middle one, of course—that you'd need a microscope to see but for which they need a Band-Aid—maybe two. Seriously, they do. They're bleeding! All this while unintentionally flipping us off.

Husband and I have gotten really good at leaving sentences unfinished and assuming the other knows what we were going to say. We *have* been married thirteen years, after all.

I won't go into all the trouble this can cause. Arguments are good for marriages.

Trips to the store together.

The last time we all went to the store together, two kids fought over who was going to push the cart and nearly tore off my toe in the process, another kid slipped three packages of chocolate chips into the basket when we weren't looking, another kid flattened himself on the bottom of the cart so he could fly and ended up smashing his finger (which I told him would likely happen), and another kid disappeared for half an hour while all the frozen fruit and vegetables defrosted because of a very hastily-organized search party. We almost left without the last kid, who was charged with watching the defrost process so he could report about it later, keeping the secret about the chocolate chips, and not moving the cart. (I dare you to guess which one of those instructions was mine.)

Never again.

Confidence.

Kids will say anything—and everything—to other people. They will tell another person how old you are (and be *way* off), how much you weigh (and also be *way* off), and how hard you cried while watching *Pete's Dragon* last Friday. They'll tell all your secrets, especially to their favorite teacher.

Good luck keeping a healthy sense of confidence with a kid who hugs you, hugs you again, and then asks you if you're having another baby because your belly sure is poking out.

The most basic form of self-care.

I'm an introvert living with six wild, loud, rambunctious boys, which means I need a daily moment—or a hundred of them—to care for myself. Reading is my favorite way to do this.

Not that I have the opportunity to do it often. When I try to put my feet up for any amount of time, someone decides it's time to open up the game closet and take out all the games that have no less than ten thousand pieces; someone else decides it's the perfect opportunity to steal into my room, where all the devices are stashed in hiding places (we're running out of unknown places, apparently), and spend some extra minutes doing the forbidden: playing with tech; and still another takes a pair of scissors to his shoelaces, his shirt, his underwear (he wants us to believe he blew out that hole with a massive fart), and, regrettably, his hair.

A nice and tidy home.

It doesn't matter how many times you remind them where hampers are, where shoe baskets are, where their school things go, kids will walk out of their clothes, kick off their shoes, and drop their school things in the hall and forget all about the after-school procedures they've done for the last four years (ironically, the oldest is the most consistently forgetful).

And by the time you've solved this problem, they've decided it's time to examine all the pencils in the pencil holder —and by examine, they mean dump them out—because anything's better than mental math.

Scissors, glue, permanent markers, paints.

Do you know what can happen if you leave a child unattended with any of the fun art supplies listed above? You will end up with a four-year-old who looks like he has mange, another four-year-old who's no longer hungry because his snack was Elmer's glue, a four-year-old (previously mentioned —yes, the same one) with permanent whiskers on his face, and another four-year-old (also previously mentioned) with an acrylic mural on his shirt (he didn't like the one that was already there.).

It's easier to get rid of them. The supplies, I mean.

Stylish clothes.

My closet has not been updated since 2006, which coincides with the year I became a mother. I am constantly buying clothes—but not for me. No, I buy clothes for the kids who walk on their kneecaps and blow out their jeans within a month of receiving them. I buy clothes for the kids who use the toes of their tennis shoes as makeshift brakes—even when they're running. I buy clothes for the kids who think "shirt" is synonymous with "napkin."

The only thing even remotely consistent about my children (besides their complaining about what's for dinner before we've sat down to eat it) is that they will require our entire clothes budget for themselves.

I'm down to my last pair of jeans. Not because they've worn out (I hardly ever wear them, to tell the truth), but because, well, things are expanding. If you know what I mean.

Sleeping in.

The beginning of parenthood had me fooled. When Husband and I only had one kid, he slept so late we could wake at a decent hour and still get things done. As the years passed and the kid-count increased, that rise-and-shine time became earlier and earlier and earlier. Now, on a school day, my kids sleep until 6:30 a.m. On weekends they sleep until 5:30 a.m., if we're lucky. We're usually not.

Sleeping in is overrated anyway.

We may give up a lot to have kids, but on our best days, we'll agree that it's worth it. On the worst days, we'll still agree it's worth it—hard but worth it. Because what we get in return —sweet kisses that miss their mark but hit the bull's-eye, hugs that hold on, a voice that whispers in your ear how much they love you—is what dreams are made of.

At least until you get on the phone with your health insurance and realize it's going to be a long afternoon in more ways than one.

New Year's Goals for Every Parent (Or Maybe Just Me)

Every year Husband and I sit down to make some goals for the new year. And, of course, this year was no different, although six boys make it a little hard to have any stretch of uninterrupted time to write out goals we can comprehend without a "decode the fragments" contraption (does anybody have one of those? Because I have all kinds of notes in journals that I need decoded, and it would be lovely to figure out what I was trying to say.).

If these goals don't make a bit of sense, I'm sorry. We're drowning here, and my life preserver has a hole in it.

1. Make one meal where no one says, "I don't like that" before they even taste it.

This every-day occurrence really ignites my annoyance. Here I've sweat over a pot on the stove for the last hour and a half and someone comes into the house, glances at the pot (he can't see over the rim), wrinkles his nose and says, "Ew. I don't like that." Sometimes it's better news: "I hate that." Sometimes it's a commentary on how amazing the dinner looks: "This looks like something you would feed pigs."

I'm kidding. My kids have never said that. Judging by the looks on their faces, though, they've certainly thought it.

This phrase and its variations are so irrational. I know my feasts don't look like food masterpieces, because I'm not a chef, but at least close your eyes and give it a try.

Usually, when one of my kids complains about what's for dinner, I say, "You can do hard things." They look at me like I'm crazy. And then they ask for seconds.

2. Put the kids to bed and have them stay there—at least once.

I know, I know. My kids should be staying in their beds every night. They should stay put, because I'm the parent.

Well, I'll tell you what. I'll trade you for a day, let you take care of six boys for twenty-four whole hours and we'll see if *you* feel like putting them back to bed three million times at the end of your day. Husband and I are done by the time bedtime rolls around. That doesn't mean we won't stop trying. It just means our trying is...tired.

Our bedroom door is a revolving door until about 8:45 p.m. (9:15 during the first month of the Daylight Saving time change), one or the other of us constantly going out to tell our sons the exact same thing: It's not time for talking or playing or turning flips in your bed. It's time for sleeping.

I wish someone would tell *me* that—not that I can turn flips anymore.

On the nights when it's really bad, Husband and I have gotten really good at pretending not to hear footsteps and laughter and knocking. We'll fall asleep with our box fan blasting and wake, minutes later, to a creepy kid standing at our bedside.

Which is not good for the heart, in case you were wondering.

3. Place recyclable items in the recycling basket—for good.

My nine-year-old is an environmentalist, and he likes to save things and reimagine how they might be used. He's invented some really amazing things—yo-yos from old baby pacifiers that break after a couple of uses, homemade hand sanitizer with old liquid soap bottles (it's actually only water with a few suds, but I don't have the heart to tell him or the people to whom he sells it for a dollar), meltable lamps from milk cartons. This desire to reuse is a great and noble thing—a value we have instilled in him.

But when he's on trash duty, it gets a little complicated.

Him: Here's a cereal box, Mama.

Me: Oh. Put it in the recycling.

Him: That's where it was.

Me: Why'd you take it out?

Him: Because it can be reused. For a book box.

Me: We already have a billion book boxes.

Him:

Me:

Him: Fine. I'll keep it, then. [He didn't even mention my expert use of alliteration.]

Me: It better not be on your floor later.

It *is* on his floor later. I put it in the recycling. And we start the dance all over again.

I love this about him. It's just that I'm not so keen on climbing into bed with a mascara container, an old Annie's bunny grahams box, and an empty clear carton of blueberries he thinks I could reuse if I "just think hard enough."

4. Leave the house without searching for shoes or cups or jackets or kids.

This is a tall order. Every time we try to leave the house, someone is missing a shoe or both shoes, which they claim they put where the shoes were supposed to go and now they're missing because someone took them. Or someone can't find a jacket that was hung up on their hook and is now not there. Or someone needs drink real quick. Or someone went missing.

Our kids make us late more frequently than they make us on time. I don't like definitive statements, but this is probably a true definitive statement: My kids make me late every single time I try to leave the house.

In the new year, I would like to leave once—only once!—without searching for something important, just to prove we can.

5. Reduce argument duration time from two hours to one.

We have in our home one of those strong-willed children (actually we have a few of them, but two are too young to be skilled at it yet, thank God.). Fortunately, this strong-willed child also happens to be a sticky-brained child, which is to say when he gets something in his brain, he cannot let it go. For hours. Possibly days.

As you might imagine, strong-willed and sticky-brained is a *very* fun combination.

He fixates on something he wants, he argues about why he should have it his way, he won't let it go for hours. You can grant him his desire in wish form ("I wish I could let you play with your LEGOs at all hours of every day. Unfortunately there is something you need called sleep."); you can repeat in robot voice, "I've already answered your question. Forty billion times."; You can explain the philosophy behind your decisions every possible way you can imagine, and he still will push and push and push.

I would like to reduce the amount of time we spend each day arguing with this kid. This likely will entail teaching him how to pick his battles (not every one is worth it, baby), how to take no for an answer every now and again, and how to use his admirable qualities of passion, perseverance, and sticky-brained-ness in a way that will benefit not just him but the whole world.

Who said parenting was easy? Certainly never me.

6. Go a week without hearing a blood-curdling scream.

I live with a pack of boys. I've lived with a pack of boys for several years now. In my living with a pack of boys, I've become convinced that screaming is their natural mode of communication. They scream to each other, they scream to us, they scream to the neighbor kid who's half a mile down the street, because they think it's faster and more effective than climbing the hill to talk to him like a normal human being.

This kind of screaming isn't going away anytime soon. So

for this goal, I'm talking more about the screaming that happens because of dangerous living. My boys are in love with dangerous living. They'll jump from their treehouse to the trampoline (who could see that coming when Husband put the treehouse together? Me. Who was ignored? Me. Who feels satisfaction now? Me. I mean, not me.) and scream when they land on their leg the wrong way. They'll bounce from the trampoline to their rock-climbing wall on the backside of their playscape and scream when they miss it completely and bonk their head on a tree. They'll all slide down the stairs head-first at the same time and scream when one boy kicks another boy in the nose (I think they're really screaming about not winning the slide-down-the-stairs race, but, whatever. Semantics.).

They scream when they nearly cut off a finger playing with a shard of glass they ferreted out to the backyard and the blood wells up like a volcanic explosion. They scream when someone turns around from falling on their face and the falling one's face is no longer tannish-white but tannish-white with red smeared all over it because of a nose that landed on a rock. They scream when they swat at the bees pollinating our flowers and one precocious bee decides to thank them by sticking a stinger into their finger.

I admit: this is probably an unrealistic goal, but I'm nothing if not ambitious.

As you can see, I have big plans for this new year. It's a good thing the common denominator in all these goals are really fickle, unreliable little human beings, because otherwise they'd be way too easy.

I've always liked a challenge.

(Ask me at the end of this year if I still like challenges. It'll be a fun experiment.)

Surprise! We're Doing the Same Thing We Did Last Night!

We're coming up on bedtime, and my boys are sword-fighting with foam swords, swinging nunchucks from between their teeth, and launching themselves at each other from the bouncy surface of their bed.

Our bedtime routine is orderly, particular, and simple. After dinner, we do chores, then we take baths, then we read stories, then we have a period of silent reading, then we pray, then we go to bed.

We've been doing this same routine every single night since we've been parents. Which means my sons have moved through this routine every single night they've been alive.

Arguably, that's more practice successfully completing this routine for some than for others. But practically every night, with astonishing consistency—no matter how long they've been alive—my sons forget what the routine looks like.

To review, it looks like this: Dinner, chores, baths, story time, silent reading time, prayers, goodnight.

Tonight, when we were collecting stories for story time, the nine-year-old apparently thought it was run-around-the-house-naked-and-see-who's-fastest time. Nope. The six-year-old thought it was stand-on-my-head-without-any-underwear-on time. Nope. The five-year-old thought it was antagonize-my-four-year-old-brothers time. Nope.

The four-year-olds thought it was play-chase-and-try-to-jump-over-pillows time and try-to-eat-as-much-toothpaste-as-we-can time and throw-stuffed-animals-in-the-air-and-watch-the-fan-slice-them time. Nope, nope, nope. And an extra nope for whatever they'll dream up next.

"Okay," I said, in my best impression of what an enthusiastic and patient mother would sound like. "It's time for stories. Remember the consequences for not sitting quietly and listening?"

No one heard me.

I said it a little louder. Still nothing, at which point I yelled at the top of my lungs, "Sit down, or it's early lights out for you."

I think I strained a vocal cord. Possibly several.

I know yelling isn't the best way to handle these wild animals, but our megaphone went missing, and I needed something effective. Mama doesn't yell a whole lot, despite what my kids will tell you. So when I do, they pay attention. Well, about two percent of the time. That's a start, though, right?

Tonight's catastrophic execution of the nightly routine didn't begin with the space between baths and stories, though. It was a roller coaster all the way from dinner. We got to chores, and everyone high-tailed it out the door, because I guess they forgot that they had to wipe the counters and the table and do the dishes and sweep and take out the trash. So Husband and I had to waste our own valuable time (who's gonna keep the recliner warm if not me?) rounding them up and reminding them of the consequences for not adequately performing their after-dinner chores, which are as follows:

1. If you leave the kitchen without performing your chore satisfactorily (as defined by Mama or Daddy), you will be assigned another chore.

2. Mama and Daddy will gladly do your chore for you (and any extra chore you have been assigned). You can pay us for our time with money from your allowance.

They moaned and complained and said things like, "My friends don't have to do chores" and "This is the worst family ever" and "We're the only kids in the whole world who have to wash dishes and sweep, and it's not fair." Their complaints added a whole five minutes to the chores time.

Still, they had some time remaining to run outside and play.

I'm always torn about letting them go play outside after chores. On the one hand, it expels some bottled-up energy. On the other (and this is based on an observation of all the nights prior to this one), there's a high probability that it will contribute to a breakdown of the nightly routine.

As it did, again, tonight.

This is how it happens just about every time we permit them to play outside after chores:

Me: Okay! It's time for baths!

Them: WHAT?!!!! (There might be a few more exclamation points than that. They're always completely shocked that they have to take a bath.)

Once we got them rounded up, they stomped up the stairs in protest. While I grabbed the baby and Husband wrangled the twins—somewhere between the time they stood at the bottom of the stairs and the time they got to the top—my older boys forgot what it was, exactly, they were supposed to be doing. When Husband and I bounded up the stairs, one of them was flipping off the chaise in the home library, one was rolling along the floor with a stuffed animal, and the third was doing sit-ups the wrong way.

Let me just interject here to say what you probably already know: we run a very tight ship in our home; it's the only way we can maintain our sanity. Our children know the schedule. Baths between 7 and 7:20 p.m., story and reading times between 7:20 and 7:50, prayer time between 7:50 and 8. Bedtime, 8:15 sharp.

Every one of those transitions is news to my sons. Every night.

And then comes bedtime.

We have consequences for not staying in bed when it's bedtime. Our boys can't seem to remember these consequences.

Tonight was one such night, because when the ship is sinking, it has to go all the way down.

After telling our boys it was time to get in bed and stay there, we heard some suspicious noises that beckoned us from our room. The nine-year-old had wandered downstairs "accidentally" to "check on a LEGO Minecraft construction."

Here's how that conversation went down:

Me: It's not time to play with the LEGOs. It's actually time to get in bed. Playing with LEGOs is not the same thing as getting in bed.

9-year-old: But I didn't get to play with the LEGOs all day.

Me: You've had a long day of playing with LEGOs. I can tell by that mess on the floor.

9-year-old: I didn't make that mess.

Me: Oh. Sorry. It must have been that other 9-year-old who lives in our house.

9-year-old: Yeah. Probably.

Me: Did you hear what I just said?

9-year-old: Yes.

Me:

9-year-old:

Me:

9-year-old: Wait.

One of these days, I know my sons will finally get used to this every-night routine—probably right around the time they leave home for college or whatever comes next for them. And I guess that's what really matters: equipping them for what comes next.

Maybe tomorrow night I'll give them a night off. Maybe we'll eat outside and won't worry about sweeping or wiping off tables, because nature does that pretty well on its own. Maybe we'll let them take a swimsuit shower out on the back deck and read stories while they jump on the trampoline and then carry them on our backs up to their beds when it's lights-out time.

What's life without a few surprises?

The Non-Conforming Child: a Humorous Tale

It is not outside the realm of possibility that other homes with children can exist without as many rules as mine. But, unfortunately, it is also not outside the realm of possibility that my home would devolve into a scene from *Lord of the Flies* if it were not governed with rules. Left to their own devices, boys would pull dirty socks from the laundry and wear them every day, never take a bath, and likely accidentally die by daring.

We have rules for everything—rules I never thought I'd have to make. But that's a subject for another day.

What I want to talk about today is how running a house with rules does one particular thing better than all the other things: It highlights the amazing strong will of the family's non-conformer.

I have a few of these non-conformers in my house, and you'll see them out and about with shirts that are not buttoned up correctly (Me, to my four-year-old twins: What is taking you so long to get dressed this morning? Both of them, in unison: We're wearing button shirts and we're buttoning them ourselves. Hey, more power to them.), shoes that likely don't match, and, secretly (or not so secretly, if you're the four-year-olds), no underwear.

There is one who is more…let's call him intense…than the rest.

It's not easy raising a non-conformer. Sometimes it's the most annoying thing in the world.

I've never been the sort of parent who expects my kids to be perfectly behaved all the time. I also have never expected my kids to be exactly the same. I know kids well enough to understand that (a) they have bad days and (b) they're all different. Maybe that makes parenting a little more challenging for me, but it also makes it more enjoyable. I get to see my kids blossom into who they are.

I have another problem as well: I'm a non-conformer. I'm the kind of person who, when someone tells me I can't do something (I'm not speaking of crimes and such; don't misunderstand me), my response is, "Watch me." I want my kids to have that same attitude—not convinced by the "experts" who say they know everything about everything.

It's just that when it comes to a nine-year-old non-conformer, things get a little tricky. Sometimes, honestly, I'd rather he just give it up and conform already. It would be easier for me.

My non-conformer walks to the beat of his own drum. He has a billion ideas in his head and a maddening urge to do them all, right now. He talks nonstop about the plans he has, the benefits of letting kids build with LEGO pieces all day every day, and Minecraft.

The most frequent word ejected from his mouth is "Why?" As a question. Sometimes as a response. All the times as a challenge to authority.

Here are some of the things we go round and round about.

Dress code

We don't ask much. At school, we just want our sons to be comfortable—which means no shorts in the dead of winter and no sweat suits in the dead of summer, which is pretty much every month but January and February here in South Texas. Other than that we only expect tennis shoes, socks with the tennis shoes (you'd be surprised how many times they forget socks, which is why my house smells like an ancient Frito factory mixed with soured sweat when I'm not proactively diffusing essential oils), and a shirt of any kind. (We've had to add a couple of amendments to this, including (1) no shirts with nipple holes you cut out with scissors and (2) underwear. Please, underwear.)

The non-conformer slides around this dress code by not tying his tennis shoes. I told him the other day that he should just take the laces out and save himself some trouble. He said, "Why?" which is the standard response any time we say anything that has the word "should" in it. I'm waiting for him to trip and bust his face (not too badly, of course), so I can say, "*That's* why." In a very empathetic and understanding tone, of course.

Church is a bit of a different story. We still don't expect much—we want them to wear jeans and a T-shirt or a nice shirt, if they so desire (they hardly ever desire). No holes in jeans, no sweat pants, no ratty clothes that make you look like a feral cat that got in a nasty fight.

The non-conformer is the kid who's dressed in sharp black dress pants and shoes that are actually tied for once and yet dons a collared workout shirt.

It's about all we can ask.

Homework

We want them to do it. Before tech time, before play time (as much as that pains me), before dinner time.

The non-conformer will fight, cry, argue, stomp for half an hour, then begrudgingly take five minutes to do his homework, because he's a whiz at all things academic. Yesterday I tried to point out that if he just sat down as soon as he got home and did it, he would have so much more time for other things.

He said, "Why?"

I shook my head.

Dinner

Everyone in our house is expected to be at the dinner table promptly after we call them. The key word is "promptly."

We will call everyone into the house, and most of my boys will be ravenously eyeing the food they just said they didn't like before they've tasted it, and there is one seat empty. Guess whose.

We'll go ahead and pray without him and dig in. He'll amble to the table five or ten minutes later and say, in a voice full of hurt, "You're eating without me?"

"We called you to the table," his daddy will say. "You didn't come."

"I was just finishing this one thing," he'll say.

"And we were finishing dinner," I'll say. I don't really say that. I say nothing, because there is no arguing with the nonconformer.

Even though he gets to the table five or ten minutes after we do, he'll still beat Husband and me to the clean plate.

Bathing

The rule in our house is you must take at least four baths or showers a week.

That might seem gross to some people, but, hey, you're not me and I'm not you. It's a way we make parenting easier on ourselves.

The problem, however, is that when boys get old enough to take a bath or shower on their own, they no longer have the drive to do so.

My nine-year-old sort of decided he was ready for showers this year. The other day he came downstairs with some stringy, greasy hair hanging down in his eyes.

"Uh, how long has it been since you had a shower?" I said, trying to count back the days. I couldn't remember.

He shrugged. "I don't know," he said.

"Go take one right now," I said.

It's not that he doesn't want to take a shower; it's just that there are more important things to think about and do. When I went upstairs later that same morning, he had not gotten in the shower. He was, instead, hovering around an old CD player listening to Jim Dale read him *Harry Potter and the Sorcerer's Stone*. When he lifted up his arms to reach for something on his desk, I nearly passed out.

And this is why we can't have a nice-smelling house.

Bedtime

Bedtime is a challenge for any kid. The days are so much fun, and they are never done playing. For the non-conformer, bedtime is merely a suggestion.

It doesn't matter how many times I lecture my non-conformer about how important the proper amount of rest is, he will look at me and say, "I just want to finish this book."

And how can a mom who is an author say no to that? It's what I hope every kid who reads my novels will say to their own parents—because it means they're interested in the story and that they are learning to love reading.

But still. Sleep.

Sometimes he'll come up with other things. "I'm going to clean my room real quick," which means, in nine-year-old terms, he's going to spread everything out that's currently on his floor (and there are a lot of things), stack it into piles and then leave it there so it can spread out evenly across the carpet again. Ever been stabbed in the cheek by the tail of a LEGO dragon because you tripped over a scarf your son had lying in the doorway of his room? I have.

Sometimes I let him stay up and clean.

Other times I'll find him sitting on the toilet, a book open in front of him.

"It's time to go to bed," I'll say.

"I know," he'll say. "I'm just using the bathroom."

For half an hour.

Going out as a family

When we're having what we call a Family Fun Day, we tell our boys they can bring a few things with them—just not all the things.

My non-conformer, however, will walk around with a backpack that is perpetually dragging him down into a sitting position. One day we were all gathered around looking at the display of dinosaur bones at the local Witte Museum, and he had his knees bent like he was using a prehistoric toilet or something.

"Straighten up," I said. "You're standing weird. People are gonna think you're…"

"My backpack's a little heavy," he said, after which he swung it from his back and opened it up. I was surprised (but shouldn't have been) to see at least ten books, a billion LEGO mini figures, and a package of brand new art pencils that were losing their points every time he readjusted. The inside of his backpack was a colorful display of accidental pencil marks.

"What could you possibly need all of that for?" I said.

He shrugged. "In case I get bored."

This has been the case since he was a little boy. We'd take him to the park down the street, walking the entire way (it's only half a mile), and he'd shove coloring books and art pads and novels into his backpack, thinking he'd sit and draw or maybe read instead of playing on the playground equipment.

He never did. He would only complain about how heavy the backpack was on the way back. I would let him carry it anyway. Natural consequences.

He never learned, though. He still carries a backpack everywhere—like to the museum today.

Later that day of the museum outing, Husband found me sitting on a bench inside the children's area, where the kids were playing dodgeball, climbing ropes (don't worry, they were made to be climbed), and pumping their legs on exercise bikes.

"What are you doing?" Husband said.

"My backpack was a little heavy," I said. "Thought I'd sit down and let my back rest for a while."

Husband tried to pick up my backpack and was nearly thrown off the bench. "What do you have in there?" he said.

I shrugged. "A few things."

He opened it up, rifling through at least three books, some *National Geographic* magazines, and a couple of writer's notebooks. His eyes were wide when he turned back to me. "What could you possibly need all of this for?" he said.

I shrugged. "You never know when you'll have a minute to yourself," I said. "I come prepared."

He shook his head and eyed the nine-year-old. Then he looked back at me. He seemed to be saying something with his eyes.

I have no idea what it was, but before I could ask him, my non-conformer plopped down on the bench next to me, unzipped his backpack and took out his notebook.

"Told you I would need it," he said, before burying his face in the blank page and writing.

You could hear Husband's laugh in the next town.

Why Movie Night Isn't the Break I Thought it Would Be

Every Friday night Husband and I take out the home projector, clear away the large mirror in our living room, and set our sons loose with a movie of their choice (appropriate for little kids, of course). We always think this is a good idea, because it will allow us to either watch the movie if we choose (as long as it isn't one we've seen a half billion times already) or maybe get a little work done.

Most of the time we opt to get a little work done.

This is almost always a bad idea.

You'd think that sitting boys down in front of a screen would be a nice little break for a parent. Our kids don't watch much television, so the screens on Friday night are considered a fun treat. And because we're parents who have not yet completely lost our idealism, we always expect to get done much more than we actually get done.

The reason for this is quite simple. It's called The Kid Wander.

I don't know if all kids wander when a movie is played through a projector and magnified on a wall in a much cooler setup than I had growing up (remember the TV built into the cabinet, mesh speakers along the side, and record player on the top? Yeah, I had one of those), but mine are masters.

Not all of my kids wander. There are, to be more precise, only two with this wanderlust. They have the same exact face and the same exact thoughts and were born the same exact day.

That's right. The Kid Wander is most successfully executed by my twins.

Even if they've just had something filling to eat, they will wander into the kitchen, thinking Husband and I aren't watching (they should know, by now, that I'm always watching. There is never a moment, even when I appear to be concentrating on whatever is displayed on my computer screen, that I'm not watching them). They will try to climb up the side of the fridge and get to the fruit basket. I will catch them in the act and send them back to the living room. They will look at the floor, shuffle back into the living room, and wait until I appear sufficiently distracted to try their luck once more.

Half the time, in the middle of a movie, someone will yell that we need to pause it.

"Why?" I always say, even though I already know the answer. It's always the same answer.

"I need to pee!" the kid will shout as he's racing toward the bathroom, having waited until the last possible second.

Did he make it? I don't think I want to know.

With six kids in the house, we pause the movie more than

we watch it. And we can never negotiate this pausing. Even if they've seen the movie thirteen times, they don't want to miss a single second of it. A ninety-minute movie is, on a typical Friday night, stretched into a one-hundred-twenty-minute movie. I think they're doing it on purpose.

Maybe that little problem could be rectified if we took a little restroom break before the movie began. Knowing my kids, though, they'd probably still have to pee midway through it. They're really good at forming habits and terrible at breaking them.

If this isn't enough to completely disintegrate a parent's concentration, there's also the constant shouting of "I can't see!" when someone decides he'd rather stand up than sit or lie down. By the third act of the movie, you have to break up full-body fights when it's the two (guess who) who can't sit still and seem to forget the last forty-three times they've been told to sit on their bottoms.

If I'm trying to watch the movie, I'm especially annoyed by these little heads popping up in different places, making you feel like you're playing a version of kid-friendly whack-a-mole.

"We didn't specialize in making glass windows, you know," I like to throw out. It's something my dad used to say when I was little. It confused us immensely.

My sons just ignore me. Or maybe they're trying to figure it out, too.

Also during the third act, the boys will usually ask for some popcorn. Husband, because he's a sucker for air-popped popcorn, will usually make it for them, even though they'll have to finish it up while watching the credits. Once they have the popcorn in hand, they'll fight about who has more—right during the climax of the movie. It's no wonder they then ask if we can "turn it back" (they don't know the proper term is "rewind," because they've never seen a VCR!). No, we can't. The movie only plays one way.

After the movie's over, there are all the blankets that have to be taken upstairs (brought downstairs by boys who were "freezing"). Someone, on the way up the stairs, will probably trip on his blanket and leave half his nose skin on the carpeted stairs (it could be worse; there could be no carpet). The blankets, on the way up the stairs, usually drag something else with them, because Husband likes the tidying method I affectionately call "Stack It On the Stairs," and now all that stuff needs to be re-stacked. On the stairs. So it can take a blanket ride tomorrow morning, too.

They'll shove each other like little wrecking balls with hands, trying to see who can make it to the bathroom first and claim the sink (there are two sinks. They forget this every night). There are hurt feelings to soothe and hurt toes to kiss and hurt heads (mine) to massage.

By the time I wrestle them all into bed and then back into bed, I'll wonder if movie night was worth it.

Probably not. The to-do list is still endless.

But in between this Friday and next Friday, I'll forget this, and I'll make all the necessary plans for next week's Family Movie Night. Because surely this time I'll be able to get a little work done.

5 Things I Didn't Know Before Becoming a Parent

Before I became a parent, I was a tense young woman whose biggest goal in life was to achieve perfection in every single thing I did. If I made a ninety-seven on a test, I would complain (and probably cry a little) because it wasn't a ninety-eight (yes, I was dramatic in every sense of the word. Husband would probably say I still am, but he doesn't know what he's talking about.). When I forgot the words to a song during the middle of a music set with our folk/rock band, I would beat myself up for the failure of my memory. When I tried anything at all, I had to do it the best that I could possibly do it.

And then I had kids.

There is something about kids that wrestles control right out of your hands. There is something about them that turns parents into different, arguably better people (most days). There is something about them that destroys everything we have known and builds it all back up better.

What I didn't know about children before I became a parent is that

They will destroy a world.

Parents, before we become parents, often have this nice little picture of the way we want things to be. We know what kind of parent we'll be in every circumstance, we know what will work for us and our currently nonexistent child, we've already planned out their lives: we'll put them on a schedule immediately and they will eat when we want them to eat and sleep when we want them to sleep and play when we say they can play. We think we'll be able to take our baby on all those outings, to all those gigs, into new and unknown places, and he will sit there all nice and happy and perfectly content to be along for the ride. We'll be able to continue our lives the way they've always been, except with a cute little child to raise.

And then we have a strong-willed child, and we realize that we know nothing about parenting, because here is a heart that still needs to be valued and protected and shaped by hands that are gentle yet firm, and it's not an easy task, because he takes our definitions and our schedules and all our expectations and tears them up in our face so those tiny little pieces float out on the winds of defeat and don't have a hope of finding each other again.

And then we take that destroyed world we thought we wanted, and we build another.

They will destroy a home.

Everywhere I look there are holes in the walls and nicks in the furniture and bookshelves with drawings on them and doors with crayon art. I don't even know what to think sometimes when I walk into my four-year-old twins' room and there's another cave painting courtesy of chalk I didn't know they had; or when one of them walks into a room I'm tidying, with a permanent marker in their hands, and I know I'm probably going to find a disaster on a wall or door somewhere. Things like this used to bother me immensely, because this is our home, and they needed to respect our home. They needed to take care of stuff. They needed to be different, mostly.

And then the nine-year-old started dealing with anxiety and depression, and we decided to take him to see a therapist, and he remembered this time, back when he was three and his second brother had just been born, when we had a decorative glass ball that he picked up in his hands and threw into the kitchen, where it shattered on the floor. He remembered, mostly, how I'd screamed one long, terrifying scream. No words, just a scream. He remembered the feelings it evoked in him.

He taught me that things aren't as important as hearts, and just because a heart considers it a good idea to doodle a name all over a little shelf doesn't mean that a heart should be broken for it—only taught. So this destroyed home, every time I look around it, reminds me that a home is not made of perfection but imperfection—memories in unintended murals on the walls and broken lights that shatter expectations and cracks that tell a story, every one of them.

They will destroy a heart.

It's when they forget who they are and we are challenged with trying to remind them, even though they have fallen so far from our "behave well" and "make good choices" and "honor all people" expectations that we don't know if even *we* remember who they are. It's when they're afraid someone is bullying them, when they have a fight with a friend they really love, when they feel alone because they're not sure anyone at school really likes them, since no one ever plays with them at recess. It's when they sign on to the narrative that they are not good enough, not worthy enough, to be loved.

Those are times a parent's heart snaps clean in two.

But it happens at other times, too. When they smile at me. When they look at me with that gleam of mischief in their eyes. When they tell me they love me and I can tell that they mean it. When I look at them and notice how much they have grown.

Nearly every single moment of the parenting journey destroys a heart. But those same moments, mysteriously, put it back together, too. Those moments tell us we are worthy of this great and brilliant love that's like a hurricane, rooting up all the parts of us that never belonged in the first place—the hurts, the disappointments, the crooked beliefs about self and others.

We learn, in this destruction, that children are the best teachers we have in the world.

We will let them.

I would never have imagined, before I was a parent, that I would one day reach a place where I would let my children destroy my life and my house and my heart like they do and be perfectly okay—content, even—with that destruction. I did not know that I would, in fact, embrace this destruction. I did not know that I would see the way destruction had shaped me into a person who is far more compassionate, far more open-minded, far more curious.

We will like it.

Who would have thought that one day I would look around my house and see a broken toilet paper holder and think about how that happened when one of my twins was trying to change the roll out himself and he used a little more force than necessary? Who would have thought the memory of this would make me smile? Who would have thought I'd hug him for his valiant and yet massively failed attempt, a year later?

Who would have thought I would see this woman I am today and rejoice that she is better, stronger, more resilient—so resilient—because of the challenge and wonder of her children?

Certainly not me.

But it's not so hard to understand.

After all, this is the shape of love.

The Fastest Way to Go Insane: Try Working From Home With Your Kids Around

Husband and I both own businesses and work from home. He runs a successful video marketing company and I run a writing business. This means we see a whole lot of each other, which is great. We get to each lunch together and hang out together, and we get to talk to each other about the crazy things our kids are doing today, and we get to tag-team on the child-raising so our sons get to spend as much time with their daddy as they do with me.

It's not lost on me how fortunate we are to do this. I'm very grateful.

We have three sons in school right now. Someone else takes care of them all day, and I'm only responsible for the three who remain at home, which is responsibility enough, since two of them are Dennis-the-Menace-on-steroids twins.

I don't usually work when I'm on duty with the kids, but lately I've been using about a half hour of my time with them in the mornings to catch up on some communication tasks and other things that have been falling through the cracks. And everyone knows that once you start making exceptions, the exceptions start to feel like a rule.

Kids, of course, have made it super easy to work from home. Everybody should try it. Especially if they like walking down the road toward insanity only to see it waving maniacally—already behind you.

Kids actually make it very difficult—if not impossible—to work from home.

For those who are considering this life change, here are some reasons why working from home is one of the most difficult career challenges I've ever faced:

1. Their definition of what is important information is terribly skewed.

They want to tell me that they had to go poop and that their poop was dark brown and stinky, but I've got an email to send, and then after I send it, I realize I've totally used the wrong word, substituted "close" for "clothes," and there's no way that magazine editor is even going to open the essay I sent along with my email, because I used to be an editor once, too, and mistakes like that aren't tolerated from freelancers.

They want to tell me what colors they used to color Elmo in their coloring book; and they want to tell me that the hole in their jeans just got bigger, while they were watching—they didn't even touch it (yeah, right); and they want to tell me that they would like me to put the baby in his high chair so he's contained, because they really want to make some snowflakes with the shape blocks, and he's crawling all over their masterpieces and messing them up.

I know all of this is important in the worlds of children, but seriously. I'm trying to work here, kids. Figure it out.

That's just for my morning on-duty time. Then comes the afternoon off-duty-I'm-now-working time.

Husband and I have an arrangement—which our sons know about—where the kids will stay out with whomever is on kid duty and will not burst into our bedroom, which is the location of our home office, while the other parent is working. And sometimes our kids do well with this arrangement; sometimes not so much. It's not unusual that they will come bursting into my room, while I'm on my working shift, to tell me that their friend has come over to play. Not life-threatening information.

Sometimes they will interrupt my work to say the grass is green, which is, arguably, something to celebrate in South Texas. Sometimes they slam in and out of the door—three or four times in fast succession—to say they had a donut right before recess today. They'll burst in to tell me that they got to play this one computer game at school and they built up a section of blah blah blah.

Now, I do love that they want to tell me all this, because I enjoy talking to my kids as much as anybody else does. But I'm also a writer. And when it's my time to write, I want to be able to write. What happens when they surprise me with a visit is that I will usually have to rewrite a thought, maybe even all the ones before it, because I require absolute concentration when I'm choosing words for a page. So a five-second interruption just cost me half an hour of writing.

2. They don't stay put.

My twins are the best escapists around. I have some amazing stories to tell on their application for gifted and talented when they go to kindergarten. They have escaped so many prisons (not really prisons; you know what I mean) in astonishing ways.

For a while, we had a lock on our back fence, which ensured that they were contained in our backyard. And then we decided that they were getting older and maybe we could try something new and see if they actually stayed where they were supposed to stay (this is always a bad idea on the part of a parent), without the suggestion of a lock—and, also, it was really annoying having to unlock the back fence when the boys' friends wanted to come follow them into the backyard and jump on the trampoline. We didn't like those friends trampling through the house because they were so numerous.

So we took off the lock. And the first day it was off, the twins escaped into the front yard (I was watching). I brought them back to sit in their booster seats as a consequence and told them that if they were going to break the rules, they weren't going to be allowed out back. We'd try again tomorrow.

We tried again tomorrow. And the next day and the next day and the next day, and every day, for two months, after that. They would not stay no matter that it meant they would be sitting in their booster seats until lunchtime and wouldn't be able to go out and play (trust me, it was probably worse for Husband and me).

So the lock went back on.

We know it's just a temporary fix, because they're the kids who figured out they could pick their bedroom lock (put in place to keep them from wandering at night and killing themselves with vitamin overdoses or worse) with the prong of a box fan. I'm waiting for them to figure out how to pick the lock on the fence, which will require a more creative solution. At least they keep our creativity flowing.

3. They like to close laptops and press buttons.

My fifteen-month-old is really good at this, because I usually like to sit on the floor so he can see me and come hug me whenever he wants. So, yeah, I know this is my fault. An email I tried to send the other day had an extra "lk" at the bottom of it. I caught it. But proofreading has taken on a whole new dimension now that the kids make it so easy to work.

My twins will randomly walk up and close my laptop, usually when I've left it for just a second because I needed to take a bathroom break or I'm changing out a load of clothes from the dryer. And, as it usually happens, they'll close it before I've saved anything, so I'll have to start over. Or the computer won't even start up because everything my twins touch turns to dust.

Fingerprint technology would be nice. It would at least delay the twins by a few months, before they figured out how to hack it.

4. You won't hear anything from them for an hour, but as soon as you're on a business call, their volume control malfunctions.

This happens more frequently to Husband than it does to me, mostly because I'm a recluse and hide away in my office so I don't have to see anyone or go anywhere or talk on the phone at all. But poor Husband. Our kids will be perfectly content playing with the wooden structures, be building a track their cars can drive down, be quietly putting together a puzzle, and Husband will see the opportunity to return a quick business call that he didn't have time to return during his shift. And as soon as he walks into the kitchen to talk, as soon as the person on the other end answers the call, the boys lose their minds.

It's a lovely, mysterious phenomenon.

5. They need something.

It never fails. As soon as I set my timer for the half hour I'm going to work (because I don't like to go over that time or it sets an unhealthy expectation for how much work can be accomplished, and before you know it your whole morning is gone), one of the kids will yell from the bathroom that he needs more toilet paper, or someone will say he's hungry, or the baby will try to crawl up the stairs.

In spite of all this, I still manage to get quite a bit done for my business during that thirty-minute window—on average, I send one email with a few misspellings. It's about all I can ask, and I've gotten used to it. So, kids, don't worry about your interruptions.

We're just subtracting it from your college savings. Which, judging by all the work I got done this morning, will be a negative balance by the time you get there.

Why Parents of Young Children Become Hermits: a True Story

Some of my friends have jokingly told me in recent days, "We hardly ever see you anymore."

And they're right.

There's a reason for this, and the reason is: kids.

I'm not one to use my kids as an excuse, but I will say that they make going anywhere difficult. If we want to meet up with some friends at a park when the first rays of light splash across the horizon (which is when my kids wake on any given Saturday), we will pay for it on the way home. If we want to go grab lunch or coffee with some college friends while our kids play on a playground, skipping right past their nap time, we'll pay for it on the way home. If we want to have dinner out with old (metaphorically speaking) double-date couples and keep the boys out past their bed time, we'll pay for it on the way home.

You might notice a recurring theme here.

Most days, it's just easier to stay home.

People often wonder why parents disappear for a time, usually that time period when their kids are young and incompetent and helpless to do anything but dress themselves, put on their shoes, and race out the door—and even that's stretching it in my house. If I want to leave to go anywhere it's almost certain that someone doesn't have underwear on, someone can't find their shoes, or someone is going to trip over the threshold of our front door and skin his chin.

Every Wednesday afternoon, we travel about forty-five minutes down a highway to get to a church and lead worship for a handful of teenagers. It's late by the time we're finished, and the kids have been cooped up in a church nursery for five hours, watching movies and eating unhealthy snacks and having everything at their disposal that they could possibly need to entertain them, besides nature.

This is a big besides.

By the time we get in the car, it's way past their bedtime, and they're so delirious they don't even know how to act. This is how that trip back home typically goes:

Boys in the rear seats: Screaming their heads off, because they're playing together. This means it's mostly happy screaming, but I still wish we had volume control.

Boys in the middle seats: Trying to talk to Mama and Daddy, even though Mama and Daddy are trying to talk to each other. Talking soon progresses to whining, which progresses to very loud crying. One of them, the baby, is asleep, a small mercy.

Mama and Daddy in the front seat: Trying to have a conversation about the church service and what's next on the week's schedule. We're not usually successful.

Over the course of the two years we've been conducting this excruciating experiment, I've captured countless conversations, taken copious notes on what boys do when they're done talking (fart and sing is about it), and calculated, on average, how long it takes before a parent feels certifiably crazy in a car with children (only about 12.8 minutes, as it happens).

Here's a typical sampling, collected this week:

9-year-old: You're a skunk.

6-year-old: Okay, did you smell that toot?

9-year-old: Yeah, that's why I called you a skunk.

6-year-old: Oh, I thought you were just calling me that.

5-year-old: Well, you are, kinda. You have white skin.

6-year-old: A skunk doesn't have white skin. It has black fur with a white stripe.

5-year-old: Well, you have a black fur right there.

[He points to the chin of my 6-year-old, which I can assure you does not have fur on it yet.]

They all dissolved into hysterical laughter, as only boys who are brothers can.

Next they started telling jokes, which was excruciating.

Knock knock.

Who's there?

Interrupting chicken.

Interrupting chicken—

[Very loud chicken noise.]

Knock knock.

Who's there?

Interrupting cow.
Interrupting cow—
[Even louder cow noise]
Knock knock.
Who's there?
Interrupting dog.
Interrupting dog—
[Dog noise that could shatter the windows.]
I thought it couldn't get any worse.
And then they started singing.

My boys are actually really good at singing. This isn't surprising; Husband and I used to be in a folk rock band before so many of them came along. We have three CDs in the archives and released a single a couple of years ago, because now that we have so many children it takes us four years to record one song. We'll be ancient by the time the next CD releases.

So the singing doesn't become a problem until the boys start fighting about which song they want to sing (as if they'll ever agree) and who actually gets to sing it (as if they can't all sing it at the same time). We suggested they sing their own songs, quietly, but the nine-year-old can't stand this sort of thing. He likes order, not chaos, and truth be told, I do too.

But, hallelujah, it was time to turn off the interior lights, which meant they'd stop fighting with each other about who was going to pick the song they sing and would start fighting, instead, with Husband and me about how they just want to finish this one thing before the lights go out.

"It's past bedtime," Husband and I said. A thousand times, a billion times. By the time our boys settled down about the lights out, we sounded like robots. And I almost wished we were.

"I only had a couple more pages!" The nine-year-old tried one more time to get us to see his way.

"You can finish it tomorrow," I said.

Actually, he finished it when we got home. He spent half an hour on the toilet reading.

By the time we get home from this weekly trip, Husband and I are usually all done with family togetherness, but still we'll have to wrestle our twins into bed, put the baby down, and remind the three older ones that it's bedtime, it's bedtime, it's bedtime.

Now it's an hour past *my* bedtime, and I'm a little grouchy.

All that work is simply not worth it. Drop by my house anytime you want. You might have to brush some spiky blocks off the couches or step over the minefield of LEGO pieces carpeting our floor, and you might want to use the bathroom before you come, but you'll always be welcome.

Just don't ask me to go anywhere with these delightful little human beings.

The Wonder of a Forgetful Kid

There's a boy in my house who requires constant, relentless reminders, even though he's ten. I'm well aware that things could change as time does its maturation work, but I suspect he may always have a tendency toward forgetfulness. That's a prediction based primarily on one fact: he's very much like his daddy.

Sometimes, when he's talking, he will forget what he's saying in the middle of a sentence, and, rather than try to figure out where he was going, he will contentedly leave it hanging unresolved for everyone else. We're either falling asleep or riveted, and both end in jarring realizations: one that he's finally finished (or is he?) and the other that we may never know what it was he meant to say. If we like neat and tidy endings, this will drive us crazy for at least an hour. Not that I know.

The other day this son came downstairs and said in a voice that could only be described as urgent with a little bit of panic on the side: "I really need you to sign my permission slip."

"What permission slip?" I said.

"The one I brought home."

"Where is it?"

He looked at me like I had tentacles growing out of my face. "I put it on the counter," he said.

I looked at the counter, where, after a week of not sorting through papers brought home from school, had a Leaning Tower of Papers (there are a lot of them around our house).

"You'll have to find it for me," I said. "I don't have time to do it." (I had a squirming baby on my hip who was begging for food.)

It would have been easier if I'd just done it myself, because by the time he was finished looking for this permission slip, there was no tower in sight. There was only a paper counter. As in, a counter made of paper

I signed the permission slip, handed it to my son, and kissed him on the mouth, even though he now prefers the cheek. Half an hour later, I found that same permission slip on the table, along with his homework. I raced the permission slip up to the school but left the homework where it was. I'm willing to let him face the natural consequences of getting a fifty on his homework if he forgets it but not the natural consequences of missing a field trip because he left his permission slip at home.

I hardly ever see this kid's school work, because he typically forgets it at school. He is the four-year recipient of the Grossest Lunch Box Ever, or he would be if such an award existed, because he forgets to bring it home most frequently and perpetually. He's the kid with the most pairs of shoes out in the van because he forgets he was wearing any once we're home from wherever we went.

He's also the kid who most consistently leaves things out and, hence, misplaces them. He will peel off his skinny jeans because he doesn't like how tight they are and I made him wear them for family pictures, and then, when it's time for said family pictures, he won't be able to find them. He will blame his brothers for stealing all his LEGO mini figures and then find them in a box in his room, where he put them before he left for school today so his brothers wouldn't mess with them. He will misplace autobiographical journals and find them buried under a carpet of books in the library (I can't be held responsible for reading misplaced journals. Just saying.).

He is the kid who brings home the most notes about missing homework, has the largest fine at the library, and needs the most plentiful number of socks. His organizational skills (or lack thereof) have cost us quite a bit of money and time over the years.

I think I might just have to get used to that.

He's ten now. The other night we went to church, and he had to bring all his new LEGO mini figures inside with him, crammed into his pockets. We were at the church a little longer than anticipated, and because his mom gets a little anal about the proper amount of sleep, we were rushing to get out of the parking lot.

We were almost to the highway that takes us home when our son said, "Oh no!" in that panicked voice he reserves for Things That Are Lost Forever. I knew what he was going to say before he said it. "My mini figure!"

"We'll be back on Sunday," Husband said. "You can get it

then."

We crossed our fingers for a docile agreement.

But this boy happens to be our strong-willed boy, too, so what we got was the complete opposite: crying and raging and calling us the Worst Parents Ever for about fifteen miles down the road, and then, for the rest of the trip home, a series of blaming exercises, during which he invented elaborate stories about which brother had been responsible for the disappearance of this mini figure.

Half an hour later, we were home. He got out of the car and stuck his hand in his pocket—the why doesn't matter; it's the what that counts.

What did he find?

The missing mini figure. It had been there, in his pocket, all along.

He smiled sheepishly, apologized to everyone he'd blamed (which was everyone in the car), and said, with a nervous laugh, "Maybe I should check my pockets better next time."

You think?

Hills I'm Not Willing to Die On

When you're a parent of irrational children (which is every child for at least a small amount of time), there are a whole lot of hills. There are hills where you will battle over which color plate is the best color plate, even if it's a color that doesn't exist among the plates stacked in your cabinet. You will battle over whether or not a plate of that color, indeed, exists inside your cabinet. You will battle over why the orange plate is the plate they're getting if they want lunch.

There are hills where kids stand with feet planted and arms crossed and say they're not going to wear the red shirt because their teacher's favorite color is blue, and they want to make their teacher happy today, not you. There are battles where kids insist they put their shoes where they're supposed to go yesterday and someone else must have moved them. There are battles during which kids will pick their nose and eat the treasure right in front of your face while claiming they don't pick their nose and eat the treasure anymore (I just saw you. Nuh-uh!).

There are massive hills and tiny hills, round hills and oval hills, rock-solid hills and mushy ones.

One thing remains the same: There are many, many hills.

These hills can get bloody and complicated, depending on the battle. But one thing I've learned in my parenting life is that if we're engaging in full-armored and weaponed battle on every single hill our children summon from the rocky ground of childhood, we're going to die on every single one of them.

So there are some hills I'm no longer willing to die on.

1. The Hill of What They Look Like

I don't care if they wear a vertically-striped shirt with shorts that have horizontal stripes. I don't care if the waistband of their pants is pulled all the way up to their shoulders. I don't care if they could walk the Pacific Ocean without getting the legs of their jeans wet because they're wearing their twelve-month-old brother's jeans.

I don't care if they didn't brush their hair today, because they're boys, and their hair's short. Knotted, but short. I don't care if they're saving that smudge of jam on the side of their face for later. I don't care if they wear one flip flop and one tennis shoe all the way to the library and back. I don't even care if they wear two left shoes, so long as the decision was theirs and they don't complain about it.

I don't care if this shirt is as wrinkled as their eighty-year-old great-grandfather's face because they like stuffing their clothes in drawers instead of hanging them up. I don't care if they buttoned up their shirt all wrong and they flail away from me every time I try to fix it.

Whatever, kid. Have your way with that wardrobe. Come back to see me when you start caring about impressing girls.

2. The Hill of Where Or When They Tantrum

I used to be super-sensitive about this. When my first son was born, I was conscious of every place, every person, every escape route my kids could take to run far away from the meanest mom ever.

If we were in the doctor's office, my son couldn't tantrum on the way back to see the doctor, whom he remembered as "the man with the woman carrying a needle," because it would disturb all the other people. If I were in the park, he couldn't melt down by the swing sets without great and near-fatal embarrassment on the part of his mother. If we were at his school, I could feel the eyes of the teachers and all the other parents upon me, and I'd consider, at great length, what it might look like—what it might say about me, as a parent—if my kid dropped to the floor and started [panic attack] kicking the ground.

Well, I don't care anymore. I've become conditioned to the tantrums, I guess.

I don't care if my kid throws himself across the mulch of the park's ground and shouts about how I'm the worst mother in the history of the world's mothers because I won't let him go one more time across the monkey bars even though it was time to leave five minutes ago and he's already drained his buffer time. I don't care about the stares I get from the other watching people, likely (or maybe not) condemning me for the way my kids are behaving, as if their behavior somehow reflects on how good or bad my parenting skills are.

If my kid's acting the fool, I'll let him act the fool (within reason, of course), because the consequences of acting the fool that will come later, when we're away from all these people, will carry a lesson in its sit-on-the-couch-and-let's-have-a-talk.

3. The Hill of They Just Broke Something

I used to be fond of things. Now I'm more fond of people.

So I don't care if my kids accidentally break something that doesn't really matter in the grand scheme of things, because those sorts of things—a lamp that is knocked over by a stuffed animal someone was really excited to find; a sconce that shattered when someone thought it would be a good idea to sword fight with brooms; a wooden chair knocked over in a game of chase conducted inside the house on a rainy day—can be replaced. What can't be replaced is a relationship lost or damaged over something as silly as an unexpected breakage.

The really important things (pictures that mean a lot, computers, valuable books) are put away where kids can't get them, and all the rest of our "things" are fair game. My fault for having them out.

This also goes for spilling, destroying, or losing things.

4. The Hill of My Kid Just Said Something Inappropriate or Embarrassing

Kids are really good at embarrassing their parents. They're good at saying words the wrong way or saying things without thinking them through. In fact, some of the things they say, they don't even have the capacity to think through.

There is a story of three-year-old me that has been told and retold in our family folklore. The story goes that when a woman my mother knew told me I was the cutest little girl she'd ever seen and, after this compliment, asked me if I wanted to go home with her, I looked at her and said, "No. You're too fat."

I was not a rude child. I was simply way too candid.

I would be mortified if one of my children said this today. My mom apologized profusely and later talked to me about the difference between truth and keep-it-to-yourself.

My kids have had The Talk. It apparently hasn't sunk in yet.

Don't ask them what color your teeth are or how old you look today or whether you look a little…chubby…in this dress. They will answer gray, four hundred twenty-three, and very much so. (This is hypothetical; I don't wear dresses.)

I no longer care about their embarrassing displays of honesty.

Yes, Mama forgot to put peanut butter on the sandwiches yesterday so all you had in your lunches was bread; go ahead and tell your teacher. Yes, Mama's legs are really hairy; how 'bout you announce it to the world, and then I can actually wear shorts outside the house unashamed. Yes, Daddy dances like a chicken in pain; be sure to tell all your friends so they ask to see the chicken-in-pain in action next time they come over.

5. The Hill of I Must Keep a Perfectly Tidy House

I saved this one for last because it has been the hardest one for me to surrender. I've died on this hill a thousand times, sometimes daily. But no longer. I will not die on this hill.

Kids come with mess. They're really unskilled at cleanup, no matter how many times we train them to do it well and efficiently. And of course we'll keep trying. But if I continue to die on this hill of I Must Keep a Perfectly Tidy House, I'm either going to sacrifice my best relationship with my kids or I'm just going to become one of those mothers who walks around talking to herself (oh, wait. I already do that.). A mother who is dissatisfied with the whole of her life. I don't want to be that mother.

So [deep breath] I don't care if he leaves his sock right next to the dirty clothes hamper. We'll have our cleanup time at the end of the day, and he'll do what needs to be done. I don't care if he takes out a sheet of art paper and then, in his concentrated state, loses count of how many pages he got out, and now the table looks like it's made of papier-mâché because (of course) he also spilled the glue. I don't care if he cuts up his worksheet from school into tiny little confetti pieces. He knows how to vacuum, and it's almost time for the motivating force of Allowance Handout.

If we're fighting every single little battle that comes our way, we're not going to win the war. We don't have enough stamina. We'll burn out halfway to the end.

So these are hills I'm not willing to die on. What are yours?

I'M TOO TIRED TO FIGHT

The Preservation Habits of Kids: An Examination

You may not know this, but my calendar proves it: every year there is a week called National Preservation Week. It's not a very well known holiday, but parents actually celebrate it all the time.

That's because kids are great at preservation.

I'm not talking about the kind of preservation that looks like kids picking up litter on the side of the road or pointing out how the landscape changes when trees are razed or urging their parents to turn off the air conditioner in the middle of a Texas June because they just read a book on global warming (this is what happens when you have a nine-year-old conservationist on your hands). These are all passions to be celebrated.

But what I'm talking about here is how skilled kids are at finding trash and turning it into delightful treasures.

Take, for example, the boxes we get from Amazon.

We are Amazon Primers. Anything I can do to keep my kids out of a store, I'll do. If that means having everything I need (with the exception of my groceries, because I'm insanely picky about produce) delivered to my door, I guess I'll do it. So we subscribe to everything. Toothpaste, soap, toilet paper, coconut oil, stevia drops, cacao nibs, almond flour, more vitamins than we probably need, skin care lotions, makeup—you name it, we subscribe to it. I would subscribe to subscribing if I could.

Because we order so much from Amazon, and because it's always delivered straight to our door in bulk, we never have a shortage of boxes to recycle—or, in the kids' opinion: to keep, reuse, and ultimately destroy (that last part isn't part of their equation; it just happens naturally).

Sometimes this is perfectly reasonable and even enjoyable, because every now and then I get a wild hair and do a fun art project with my sons, wherein we'll decorate a box for somewhere around the house and watch it, day by day by day, get further demolished by the flailing legs of wrestling boys.

But sometimes, like when we get an enormous box for all the other boxes, because, apparently, this makes it easier to ship, this is not perfectly reasonable or even enjoyable. Mostly because I'll be the one to trip over that humongous box and bust my face on the side of the couch—which, you would think, is well padded. Well. It isn't. See if you're well padded after having five boys flip over you at 6:30 p.m. every evening when they should be doing chores.

My nine-year-old is probably the most passionate environmentalist in the house. He will keep everything. He's been making a little money working with his daddy on some video client projects; he wants to be a cinematographer and

Husband's trying to introduce him to the world of video recording. With this hard-earned money—which is mostly paid for arranging lights and cropdusting all over the tiny room because he's nervous—he's been buying all sorts of Pokémon cards.

He likes to keep his Pokémon boxes, because he "might need them someday." And, besides, they can be reused for a pencil collection site on his bedroom desk.

Hey, as long as it's not in my bedroom or the family living areas, go for it.

But now the other boys have gotten in on the act. They've made some tiny trees out of logs and grass in the backyard, and they want to bring these "treeple" in, because they can't get rid of the logs, which are really the charred remains from the outdoor fireplace we don't ever use in Texas because it's a thousand degrees most days and nights of the year.

And then, when one of them is on trash duty, they'll argue about what we throw in the trash, because, of course, it can all be reused for something useful—like a collection box for socks (already have a bin) or a rubber band holder (I'd really rather not) or a receptacle for preserving diapers (why would you...?).

The worst preservation my sons do? The papers.

My kids are very artistic kids, in that they will create all hours of the day. If creating were homework, we would not have our every-single-day fights, because they would gladly sit at the table and draw a line on a piece of paper and call it finished (if you're the four-year-olds). And they'll want to keep every single masterpiece.

It doesn't matter if they're only four and this "fox" doesn't really look like a fox, and they'll be better at it in another three years. They want to keep it now, because they're sure their future self will appreciate it. The six-year-old doesn't care that the piece of paper he just dumped from his red school folder was a quiz where he circled the answers, and the only evidence that it's his is the name at the top of it; he'll want to keep it to remember what his "handwriting was like." The nine-year-old has a mad scientist's stash of plans for the house he'll build someday, and no amount of persuasive arguments will take those papers and slip them into the recycling bin (he's a persistent kid, so he knows how to deal with persistent parents).

I'm trying to swim through the papers, but my head keeps going under.

I guess I should be glad I'm living with six preservationists, but it does get annoying every now and then. Except when someone sees that gigantic Amazon box and wonders what it would be like to ride down the stairs—because I actually fit in it, which means, you guessed it, I can ride down the stairs in it, too.

Who knew preservation could be so ~~dangerous~~ fun?

Fact: Kids Do Almost Everything Slowly

I almost titled this essay, "Kids Do Everything Slowly." But then I thought about how quickly my boys get into a fight with each other and how quickly that fight escalates and how quickly they run away toward me so they can be the first to tattle with their skewed story. I thought about how quickly they run anywhere and how quickly their rooms become a disaster area and how quickly they start arguing about whether or not tech time is actually over. It's not accurate to say they do *everything* slowly. Some things they do astonishingly quickly. Stealing your heart, for one.

I know that's cheesy. Bear with me.

We work really hard on autonomy in our house. Usually, it's not a problem when my sons take half an hour to sweep the kitchen floor, because everyone else will move on to some other activity while the floor sweeper is still figuring out that dancing with a broom and sword-fighting with the broom and riding the broom like a horse do not, in fact, sweep the floor to his parents' standards.

And in the several years we've been parents, Husband and

I know one truth better than all the others: Kids do almost everything slowly.

The problem is really when we have a deadline to be somewhere, and the kids aren't cooperating, because they want to do everything themselves.

I'm all for doing everything yourself. If I don't have to find your shoes, that's fantastic. I'd rather not search all over the house for the random places those shoes could possibly be, even though everyone has a basket with his name on it.

The most annoying slow things my kids do include:

1. Brushing their teeth

It doesn't matter if we only have fifteen minutes on the schedule for brushing teeth; my kids will go significantly over that fifteen minutes every single time. And it's not for actually brushing their teeth. I wouldn't have much to complain about if it were; I'd rather they brush their teeth for at least a minute or two. Fifteen would be a dream.

The bulk of their fifteen-minute teeth-brushing time is spent shoving everyone off this one stool we have in their bathroom. Only three people actually need to use it; the three others are tall enough to reach the sink without a stool. But everyone wants to use the stool. Everyone wants to stand on that step and shove everybody else off. I have a theory that they do this for the fun of it; boys are always ready for a brawl, or at least the ones in my house.

As soon as we announce that it's time to brush their teeth, you can bet you'll see them all elbowing each other to get into the bathroom first so that they will be King of the Stool.

Between their fighting and our telling them to quit, seventeen minutes have passed. They'll brush their teeth for three seconds and be done with it.

I guess we need more bathrooms. Or maybe just a good rotation system, but that would require organization, so…

2. Reading

When I have to sit down with the kid who's just learning to read, I can actually feel my teeth falling asleep. He will read one word at a time, sounding out each word using the phonics I taught him at four. Yes, of course it's super exciting that he is learning to read, but it's not super exciting that I get to be the one sitting down to listen to him learn how to read. Husband will usually save this duty for me, because he says I'm the one who taught them to read; he doesn't know how to correct them.

Yeah, right. That sounds like a copout.

If my son reads any slower, I could slip away outside, clean out our entire van—which is disgusting—and make it back in time to hear him read the last line on this same page. It's like when they're talking. Which brings me to

3. Telling a story

My sons have very unique speaking personalities. I've written an essay about this before, and you should totally read it sometime. I'll provide some of it in summary here, however. One of my sons will start over every time he messes up what he's trying to say, which means that by the time he gets to the fifteenth word he wants to say, if he messes up that fifteenth word, he will start over, from the beginning, with the fourteen words he managed perfectly well. It takes years to get out of him what he wants to say; we're still having a conversation with him about that one time he tried the monkey bars when he was three. He's five now.

Another son simply forgets what he wants to say in the middle of the sentence and blames it on whichever brother is closest to him, who wasn't even talking but was only looking at him. Another takes the longest pauses in the history of pauses and makes you think he's actually done, and then he'll start up again in the middle of a sentence. As you might imagine, this makes it seem like he is never, ever done. And he hardly ever is.

Another uses twelve billion words where sixteen—sixteen words, not sixteen billion words—could possibly have sufficed. Another of them talks in circles, never really coming to any point at all, just throwing out random observations and stream-of-consciousness thoughts. He'd probably make a good president.

By the time my day is done, I usually have a touch of vertigo from all the words that have barreled my way since my boys got done with school. Sometimes I wish I had a life-sized doll of myself that I could hand to them when they feel themselves turn conversational.

I love that they talk to me. But is it necessary to use so many words and take so long in the telling?

I'm sure they'll get better as they get older. At least I tell myself this in order to live.

4. Understanding

Kids also take an excruciatingly long time to understand anything. Sometimes I wonder if this is the difference between female and male. I'm the minority in our house; I'm approaching things from the perspective of one planet and they're approaching things from another—or at least that's what it feels like most of the time. Husband could grunt something that makes no sense at all to me, and all the boys will agree and understand completely.

I, on the other hand, could explain every known way there is to explain that "not putting your elbows on the table would reduce the likelihood of people's drinks getting spilled" and "chewing with your mouth closed is much more polite" and "there is a time and a place for when farts are funny," and they still won't understand what I'm talking about.

5. Getting dressed

My sons prefer to dress themselves. I prefer to let them.

The problem is, it takes so long for them to pick something out and then put it on. And this isn't just because they didn't put their clothes away after the last laundry day and, instead, shoved them all in a drawer, which they now cannot open. It's also because they will pick out one thing, try it on, and decide it's probably not casual enough.

This is not the only reason they dress slowly, however. My boys will also get distracted while they're dressing. They'll put on their pants, and then they'll notice that one of their brothers is reading a comic book, and they'll wander over to read it, too, even though the rest of their wardrobe is waiting for them to pull it on and walk out the door fully clothed.

6. Putting on their shoes

One of the most torturous things a parent can do is tell their kid to put on their shoes and then wait for the kid to do it himself. I will watch for twenty minutes while one kid argues with me about how he's putting his shoe on the right foot, and then when he's finally shoved it on, with a whole lot of brute strength, and tries to get up and run, he notices something is amiss. That's because they're on the wrong foot, like I've said for the last twenty minutes. He will look at me, look down at his shoes, and continue walking, because this four-year-old doesn't back down.

Good for you, kid. Have fun running in shoes that are on the wrong foot.

One of my boys is also learning to tie his shoe. We don't want to discourage him from practicing this, so every time we're getting ready to leave and he wants to tie his own shoes, we say an enthusiastic yes.

Forty-five minutes later, he has the first shoe tied.

Hey, that speaks to perseverance. But we'll go ahead and tie the second shoe.

The other day I took all my boys out to buy flip flops, because I was wasting too much valuable time waiting for them to tie their shoes (or not tie them if you're the nine-year-old and you're too lazy and you like risk-taking behavior) and it's summer. They don't need tennis shoes anymore. Sweaty feet is not my favorite thing.

It still takes them twenty minutes to slide on their flip flops. I don't understand it at all.

7. Leaving the house

It doesn't matter if they've gotten a look-ahead warning like this one: Twenty minutes until it's time to leave.

They will never be ready to go on time.

Husband and I pad our leaving time by about half an hour, and we usually leave on time or about five minutes late, because someone is always going to forget something and need back in the house. The nine-year-old is usually so engrossed with the LEGO Minecraft creation he's building that he can't tear himself away long enough to pack whatever he's going to need—which is practically our entire library, all of his art supplies, and every journal he currently owns that has at least one page available for writing.

This kid is the one most likely to make us late.

But there have been other kids who, on their way out the door, completely forget what they're doing and remember they had intended to pour themselves a giant glass of milk.

Sometimes, if we're really lucky, the kid who's pouring the milk will spill an entire gallon all over the kitchen floor, himself, and any brothers who were curiously watching.

Leaving the house is a challenge every time.

8. Cleaning up

When I tell my boys to clean up, I set a timer for fifteen minutes. There is nothing in my house that would require more than fifteen minutes to clean it up thoroughly. We don't collect a lot of things, because I don't like clutter, and when my boys are playing, they typically only have one thing out at a time.

But fifteen minutes is not enough for them.

The problem is that my kids don't think they can possibly clean anything up without playing with it while they clean. They'll be shoveling renegade LEGO pieces onto the LEGO mat, and as soon as they finish with one scoop, they'll find the piece for which they were looking earlier, and they'll tinker. They'll tinker while I say, "Ten more minutes, guys," and then "Eight more minutes to have it all cleaned up" and "Two more minutes or you're losing LEGOs for today and tomorrow," and then, when the one-minute mark is announced, they clean like mad. Unfortunately for them, they rarely make it.

It doesn't matter if there are only four LEGO pieces on the floor or there are four thousand. Fifteen minutes is simply not enough time for boys.

I don't mind that my kids are slow at practically everything. In fact, sometimes it reminds me to slow down and enjoy life a little more. I'm forced to pay attention and stay present in this place of slowing down, and I can't help but think that is a good place to be.

But velcro shoes might be good for that kid who takes forever to tie a shoe. After all, the longer someone takes to tie a shoe in our house, the more likely he will get left behind.

Not that we've ever done that.

Yet.

What Happens When You Watch a Movie Kids Have Already Seen

Every Friday night, Husband and I treat our boys to a Family Movie Night. They don't watch a whole lot of television, unless they're at the grandparents' house (that's okay, Mom. You can take them any time you want.), so this night always feels like a special occasion.

Sometimes Husband and I will sit on the couch and snuggle with our boys during the movie. Sometimes we'll take the opportunity to catch up on a bit of work that needs doing, while the boys laugh their way through the newest Pixar release. This means that sometimes our boys get to watch a movie before we do.

The most recent movie our boys watched without us was *The Good Dinosaur*. Husband and I were trying to get ready for a book launch, so we sat in the kitchen while our boys crowded on the couch and asked for popcorn. They laughed through so much of the movie and were entertained by the whole of it; I knew it was one I wanted to see.

So, another week, Husband and I sat down to watch it with them.

We settled onto our couch, and I tried to ignore the elbow that was jabbing into my side. It didn't take me long to forget that annoyance in light of another. It soon became quite clear that I would not be able to watch *The Good Dinosaur* without a running commentary from all three of my older sons.

"Don't worry. This isn't where he dies, Mama," one of them said early on in the movie, during a particularly tense part where a dinosaur is trying to outrun a storm. "He dies in another place."

Well, thanks for letting me know he dies at all. I appreciate the spoiler. Maybe I should go ahead and cry now.

Not only would they spoil just about every tense scene in the movie, but they would also insert things like, "Watch this," as if we weren't already watching the screen, and "This is a funny part," as if we wouldn't know we were supposed to laugh, and "He's not very nice," as if we couldn't figure it out for ourselves.

They would explain jokes to us and tell us what was happening or would happen and introduce characters before they'd introduced themselves on the screen, and it was like having my own personal narrator, which would have been nice if I were visually impaired, but I could see the screen just fine, and the only thing my kids' commentary did was make it really hard to hear what was said during the movie.

I get it. My sons had already seen the movie, and they remembered every part where they felt a little afraid or a little sad or a little concerned. They didn't want us to go through the discomfort of that. They didn't want us to feel as shocked as they felt when someone died or as sad as they felt when someone remembered the someone who died. They were simply warning us. It's sweet, when you think about it.

It's just that I'd like to watch a movie, please. I'd like to enjoy the tension of not really knowing what's going to happen. I'd like to hear the dialogue the first time it's executed. I'd like to be surprised now and then.

But I guess I do sort of get to be surprised, because I remember that, at one point, a boy said, "There's another storm coming," so I was waiting, on the edge of my seat, to see if someone else gets hurt in a storm, and it turns out the storm wasn't coming for another forty-five minutes. So I got to sit on the edge of my seat for forty-five minutes. There's nothing like sitting on the edge of your seat for forty-five minutes, let me tell you. I got a ridge line in my cheeks, I was clenching so hard.

Still, at the end of the day, I have to admit that watching a movie with my sons is one of my favorite things we do as a family. To have a seventy-five pound kid crawl into your lap because this part makes him a little nervous is priceless. To have a four-year-old snot your leg when he doesn't want to get up to get a tissue because he doesn't "want to miss this part" is priceless. To have a five-year-old whisper in your ear that the dinosaur makes it back to his family in the end (whoops. Sorry about that. Spoiler alert!) is priceless.

During the movie, I learned that my boys are quite proficient at play-by-plays. They're so good at it, in fact, that by the end of the movie, I became good at something, too: The

Art of Not Listening to My Children. For those of you who haven't learned how to do this yet, I just sort of turned off the ear that was facing the boy sitting next to me. He didn't seem to notice, because the drone in my right ear kept right on buzzing.

I figured out that this is the very same skill I use when the nine-year-old starts talking about Pokémon or Minecraft.

The skills you hone during Family Movie Night. Priceless.

I've Become a Parent Who Doesn't Care

I used to care a whole lot about everything. And I mean everything. I was quite a terrorist, if you ask Husband and my firstborn son. I used to care what people thought about me and my parenting choices. I used to care about what my kids looked like, because, of course, they always had to be dressed impeccably—in the right shoes and the right shirts and the right pants, with their hair styled just so. People needed to know we were handling our reality so they didn't judge us more harshly for it.

I used to care about getting places on time and how we looked walking the streets of our city and what my kids' behavior said about me.

I know better now.

My kids are their own people, and while I'm the shepherd who guides them in their journeys, they are not exact replicas of me (nor would I want them to be; I'm far from perfect, too.).

What I have realized in my years of parenting is that I often care too much about what other people think. So I resolved to stop caring.

Here are the top things I stopped caring about:

1. What others think about how many children swarm around me and call me Mama.

We get a whole lot of stares when we're out in public, and we're out in public a lot, because we like doing things together as a family. And I get it. We have a lot of kids, and they're all boys. We're quite a sight to see, honestly. I've started telling myself that people are staring at us because they're never seen boys so well behaved before (this usually happens right before one of them does something like trip another one so the unfortunate one scrapes all the skin off his chin and I don't have a Band-Aid, because I still haven't learned to carry a first-aid kit in my purse).

Every now and then, however, someone walks up to us intent on shattering my idealistic perception, because the judgment is practically dripping from their eyes. "These all yours?" they'll say. They already know the answer. We will politely answer, yes, they all belong to us.

"My God," they will say. "Ever heard of birth control?" or something along those no-filter lines, at which point we'll walk away, because our kids deserve better than that. They really are good boys. And we're hard-working, intentional parents.

So I've stopped caring about what people think about my choice to have half a dozen kids. They can think what they want. They can think I'm ruining the planet because I'm contributing to overpopulation. They can think I'm irresponsible and selfish in this irresponsible and selfish choice. They can think it's just a waste of space in our overcrowded society. They can think I'm crazy or ignorant or unschooled or back-woods or ridiculously ridiculous.

I don't care. I know who I am. And it's not who they say I am.

2. Whether or not others could handle my reality.

Recently I read an essay urging the moms of the Internet to stop being so sensitive to the things that people say about and to them. Maybe it's true that sometimes we get a little sensitive about the things people say. But I like to think that I can always tell when people mean well and when they don't. There's something in the eyes. I've always been good at reading the eyes, because I was a political reporter for a while, and a political reporter has to be really good at discerning when someone's lying to them. I'm also hyper-empathetic, which lends me a proficient insight to what people are saying when they're not actually saying it.

The people who mean well look at my family with a little more grace and joy. And I will let them joke with me all day about how I have a basketball team with a sub and how I must have been trying for a girl and how there are so many of them, everywhere—because I can see in their eyes that they mean well and they're actually quite delighted to have seen this spectacle today.

But the ones who don't mean well should just stop talking.

It's often that we will hear from people, "I don't know how you do it." Mostly it's said out of admiration, but every now and then, there's a crazed person who makes a beeline for our family when we're crossing Alamo Plaza in the great city of San

Antonio, just so they can say, "I can't imagine having that many kids," and look at our kids like they're some kind of monsters who will take over the planet and eat the brains of all the much-more-capable-and-desirable adults.

I'm not a big fan of my boys standing in front of a person who makes them feel like there's something wrong with who they inherently are, just because there are six of them. The oldest is getting old enough to pick up on this hint of scorn.

But you know what? I don't care any more if some people think they could never imagine doing laundry for six kids every week or teaching six kids every day or feeding six kids every hour. I don't care if they think I was a nutcase for choosing this kind of life for myself. I don't care.

Close your mouth and move along. This is family time. Not let's-see-what-a-stranger-thinks-about-all-these-children time, despite what you may think.

3. If the way my kids dress make them look like fashion experiments gone wrong.

My kids dress themselves. This means that many times, they don't have matching shoes or they're wearing one flipflop and one tennis shoe, because their solution for "I can't find my other Iron Man tennis shoe" is to leave one tennis shoe on and let the other foot air out with a fluorescent green flipflop.

They have holes in their jeans, because they walk and run and jump on their knees a little more than half the time they walk and run and jump. They have unbrushed hair, because they can't be bothered to put a comb through their morning mop and they're boys; who cares? They have smudges on their faces because they're magnets for dirt (which, on a side note, makes my house a magnet for dirt, too).

All of this doesn't mean we don't take good care of them. It just means kids get to dress however they want (with gentle suggestions from Mama and Daddy sometimes) and deal with the consequences of their choices. If they decide to wear shorts in forty-degree weather, they'll have to brave the cold.

So I don't care what other people think about what my kids look like. I don't care if they think we're not taking care of them or if they wonder whether we're those crazy people who don't bathe our kids every day (we don't). I don't care if they think I'm a negligent mother (I'm not) or if they think I have no style (they'd be correct; I don't have much) or if they think my kids just get to run around like hoodlums outside all the time (yeah, mostly) because of the way they dress.

4. What people think my kids' behavior says about me.

It's amazing to me how much people forget about the day in, day out battles of raising children. I've heard parents who have already raised their kids condemn current parents of young children because kids shouldn't have tantrums, kids shouldn't talk back, kids shouldn't be anything other than perfectly well behaved.

They've clearly forgotten what it's like to have young children.

So my kid had a tantrum. Stop giving me the stink-eye. So my kid didn't want to leave the park and kicked some of the mulch so it got in his twin brother's eye. Yeah, that's not allowed, but you know what? It happens. He's only three.

Emotions can't be controlled perfectly all the time. And just because I understand that doesn't mean he's not going to deal with the consequences of his actions, but it does mean that I'm going to first empathize with my kid about how hard it is to leave a park when we're having fun.

So my kid won't stop whining and it's super annoying. Mind your own business and let me take care of it.

I don't care if people think I'm too strict. I don't care if they think I'm too lenient. I don't care if they think I'm probably not the best one for this job. I don't care. I'll parent my kids however I want to parent them, because I'm the one who knows them best. I know their tendencies and their struggles and their pitfalls, and, most of all, I know their hearts.

I don't care what other people think about us anymore. I don't care if you hate families and despise children, because you think they have nothing to offer the world. I know who we are, and I know who my kids are, and I know how much value they have to offer the world, and I know that they will one day change this world they're living in—for the better.

That makes me glad I have six of them to raise.

Hoarders: Kids Edition

I'm not a hoarder. Not even close. In fact, I'm probably the opposite of a hoarder. I periodically like to assess a room and take all of the unnecessary things out of it and just throw it away.

But my kids? Well, they're a different story altogether.

They hoard stuffed animals.

For Easter this year, the kids were talking about all the amazing toys their friends were getting from the Easter Bunny. It seems like the Easter Bunny has turned into a second Santa in many kids' lives. Fortunately, we don't do the Easter Bunny, and Mama and Daddy are much higher on the cheapskate scale than the Easter Bunny that visits my kids' friends. So the boys got a five-dollar gift card to a local yogurt shop (which ended in a GREAT family outing, let me tell you) and another five-dollar one to Hobby Lobby.

I had high hopes for the Hobby Lobby card. We're always running out of art provisions, and I thought that's what my kids would head for. But no. In we walked, and they headed straight for the Beanie Boos display and then, after picking up every single Beanie Boo on the shelves and exclaiming over its cuteness, proceeded directly to the checkout counter with one in hand.

It's not like they don't have a billion already. But they hoard stuffed animals. Every time they have money, they want to buy another one. These things are like rabbits, multiplying at every turn. I've tried to get rid of some of the old ones—the ones that are too beat up to even recognize anymore because the four-year-old twins went through a de-fluffing stage—but the boys started crying like someone had died. "We can't even have a fake dog?" they said.

Well, tell me if you'd argue with that one.

"They're all loved," they say. Which is a nice sentiment. Except there's one that's been caught in a backyard tree for about three weeks, and no one's made a move to bring him back in.

They hoard papers.

Papers are my nemesis. I have three boys in school, and the number of papers they bring home is nothing compared to the number of papers they find and draw on at home. I'm sorting through about three hundred papers a day, and that's not an exaggeration. And I have to be stealthy about when I put the papers I don't want in the recycling bin, because if boys see me? It's "I made that for you. You don't want it?" and then I'm feeling guilty for even being alive.

They hoard bug carcasses.

Any time my four-year-old twins go outside—which is a lot these days, because twins are hard—they're digging holes in the yard. They are fascinated by worms and pill bugs and ladybugs, and because it's been a beautiful spring here in Texas, there are plenty of bugs to choose from. The problem is, they steal mason jars and fill them with bugs and then stock them in the pantry, so the next time I reach for the raw sunflower seeds, I'm met with a prop from a horror movie. But when I want to throw them away, my twins say the jar is full of their pets.

"They're *my* pets," one of them will say.

"No, they're *mine*," the other will say.

While they're fighting about it, I dump the contents of the jar in the trash and have plenty of time to relax, because it'll be about an hour before they've settled it.

They hoard LEGOs.

It's been a while since we introduced LEGOs into our house. And I'm so glad we did. I love having to nag my nine-year-old to clean up his LEGOs every other minute, because he gets so focused on a building project he doesn't care that it's time for dinner, he just wants to keep building.

LEGOs are great. Even I enjoy building with them sometimes, when the kids aren't home to tell me how I'm doing it all wrong. The problem is, my kids are always talking about how they want more, more, more. Have you seen how many LEGO sets there are? We would need another house to collect them all, but the nine-year-old has a mission that sounds exactly like that, with a slight addendum: "Collect them all. By the time I'm ten."

They hoard nature.

Here's a ridiculous admission for you: when I'm doing laundry, I never check the pockets. I know I should. It's really dangerous not to, but when you're separating a weeks' worth of laundry for eight people, you don't really have much time to do pocket-checking. Periodically, I'll have a load going in the washer and hear a terrible thumping noise. At first I'll think it's someone trying to break into the house, because what can I say about my imagination except that it's highly active. And then I'll realize it's coming from the washer, so I'll think the washer is probably breaking, great, now what are we going to do, there's no way I'll be able to wash clothes the old-fashioned way for all these people.

But then I'll open the washer and see the source of all that clunking: rocks.

Don't ask me why I didn't *feel* the weight of those rocks when I was sorting the clothes. That's a ridiculous question.

It's not just rocks, either. It's sticks in the bathtub and leaves all over the front entryway. My kids are hoarders.

I like a simple home, but kids make it anything but simple—not just in the emotional sense but in every other sense. It doesn't matter how many times we explain to our kids that a lower number of "things" makes us much happier, they want more. It's human nature. They have to learn themselves that things are not what will make them happy in the end. And they'll learn that eventually.

In the meantime, let's just all pretend I'm on an episode of "Hoarders" and call it a day.

How Many Baths Do They Really Need?

I have a confession to make: I don't always make my children take baths.

In fact, we're a family that bathes every other day. I could tell you it's for environmental reasons, and it is, partially, but the other big reason we don't make our children bathe every single day is that there are not enough hours in the day, and I would rather be sitting around a table doing art with my kids than trying to wrestle them into the bath, cleaning up their flood, and lecturing them on the importance of washing under their arms.

If you have never experienced the delight of a child bath, you are in for a treat. Baths in my house are very much like wrestling matches, and no one is happy by the time it's all over, because they don't ever want to get in the bath, no matter how much they enjoy it, and, in an ironic turn of events, they also don't ever want to get *out* of the bath, no matter how much they complained about tonight being bath night.

They don't fight *only* because they don't want to get in or out of the bath. They fight because they know what comes after baths—reading time and then the dreaded bedtime.

Sometimes, I don't have the energy to enter this wrestling ring.

Maybe you think I'm crazy for calling it what it is. Maybe, in your house, bath time is a wonderfully relaxing time when you can enjoy your child, who sits perfectly still and never dumps cups of water on the floor when you aren't watching. Maybe your child doesn't try to put soap in his brother's mouth when you've turned your back to prepare their toothbrushes. Maybe bath time doesn't make you feel like you sat in the first row of Sea World's killer whale show by the time you're finished.

Here's a sampling of the typical bath time in my house.

Me: Time to get in the bath! [Cheerful voice that makes bath time seem much more enjoyable than it is]

Everyone: No! I want to keep coloring!

Me: I'm sorry. I wish I could let you keep coloring. But right now it's time to get in the bath.

They complain about how all their friends don't have to take baths every day, and I tell them they don't have to take baths every day either, just four times a week, and they start complaining about how even that is too much.

"It's bath time," I repeat. They look at each other, frozen for a moment in time.

All mayhem then breaks loose at the table, because my children are all trying to be the first ones in the bath, because they all like different temperatures and depths for the water, and there is an unspoken rule among them: whoever is first in the bath gets to control the faucet. They stampede upstairs, and I watch from below, hoping no one will be shoved back down and break his neck on stairs.

It's a treacherous thing to be a mom of boys. I'm reminded of this several times a day.

Once they've all made it safely up the stairs and into the bath, someone forgets to put down the stopper, so the water is continuously running but not filling. Half of them are complaining about this predicament, assuming that the one in control of the faucet put the stopper down. I enter as the heroine, after they've already wasted forty gallons of water and there is no standing water in the tub, and put the stopper down, and then they all start complaining about the temperature of the water—except the one who is controlling the faucet. It's too hot for some and too cold for others.

How many kids are in this bath? you might be asking.

Nearly all of them. It's just easier.

The tub fills, we scrub the boys like they're on an assembly line, and then we set a timer and let them play for five minutes.

There are no bath toys in the tub. You can read about why in another book I've written, *The Life-Changing Madness of Tidying Up After Children*. So my kids, ever inventive, play with water.

By the time the timer clangs, there's more water outside the bath than inside it. I'm waiting for the day that all of us fall through the floor and into the garage, which is right below their bathroom.

Then I say, "It's time to get out of the bath."

Everyone: No! I want to stay in the bath!

This is not a battle I would enjoy having every day. It's not even a battle I enjoy four times a week. Maybe we'll start taking baths once a week.

I'm just kidding. Don't get your outrage in a wad.

I know what people think about "those parents" who don't make their children bathe every night. They think it's gross. They think we should enforce an every-night rule.

I don't really care. We don't smell at all. The only reason flies like to follow us around is because a bunch of boys live in our house, which means that when we go out and about, we carry with us the smell of all those boys. It's a combination of fart, stinky feet, and underarm stench.

Maybe that's reason enough to take a bath every night, in your mind. In that case, we're not the same, you and I. I've had six nine-year-olds in my house for a sleepover, and I have never smelled such powerful, offensive smells as I did that night. So either other boys are only taking four baths a week or it's just the smell of boy.

The nights that my boys don't have to take a bath, we can usually be found extending our reading aloud time or doing art together or planning for the next brother's birthday party or talking about the upcoming Family Fun Day and what they might want to do. I'd much rather be doing this than wrestling a wet, slippery one-year-old into a bath he doesn't want to take or listening to two four-year-olds whine in unison—with perfect pitch, even.

My boys are young, so I'm sure this four-times-a-week

practice will change when they start getting interested in girls and decide they should probably start showering every day—but that's also a time when they will not want or need their parents supervising their bath time.

You really think I get a shower every day?

Not even close.

(In my defense, this is not laziness on my part. I would like to take a shower at least every other day. But the last time I left my four-year-old twins alone for a five-minute rinse, they colored each other brown with a permanent marker I had no idea we had. And the last time I tried to bathe for ten minutes in our garden bathtub that hardly ever gets used, the six-year-old ate twenty pieces of Halloween candy and didn't think to hide the evidence of wrappers in the trash can so when I went to throw away my green tea bags, I saw them waving at me on the top of the pile. My stomach dropped when I saw them, because I thought it was Husband, and I was feeling really betrayed, because we'd made a deal not to eat all the Halloween junk. Good thing it wasn't him. I went easy on the six-year-old. I'm a terror when I don't get chocolate and Husband does. It's not fair.)

Bath time is not a matter of clean or dirty in my house. It's really, simply, a matter of survival. And my boys will survive even if they only take a bath four times a week.

Just like I'll survive having my [redacted] shower(s) a week. (Redacted because…well, you don't want to know.)

The End of a School Year: a Tale of Decline and Failure

The rapid decline of focus and care that families experience at the end of a school year is not always a sudden decline. For some people, it's a steady one that takes months and months to reach complete burnout. For some it never happens at all.

But if you're an overachiever like me, this decline requires only a few weeks before you're gracefully accepting the Failing at School Award.

Husband and I do fairly well at the beginning of every school year, for at least the first couple of weeks. Everyone has matching shoes when they get to school. No one forgets their backpacks. Sweat pants, which are part of my boys' daily wardrobes, don't have holes in them yet.

And then my boys get really tired of being in school, and they become a bit more to manage. Husband and I don't really have the time for "a bit more to manage." And it starts weighing on us in increments: so many folders to sign, not enough pens that work, so much reading time spent with kids who take ten minutes to sound out four sentences.

We start giving up.

So by the time we get to the end of the year, our failures have accumulated in massive quantities. Recently I noticed it in the frequency with which our boys showed up at school the day of their field trips with no signed permission slips.

I won't tell you how many times this happened, but, for context, we have three boys in school. The number of no permission slips was greater than the number of boys in school.

Don't ask me how that happened; I'm still confused, too.

Half the time, I did not even see these permission slips. My sons' teachers emailed me the day of their field trip or field day or movie day, asking me if I'd let them go or play or watch, and, if so, just send a note with the boy. If they only knew how hard it was to find a pen. I wrote my notes in crayon.

We missed all the teacher appreciation activities this year, not because we don't appreciate our sons' teachers but because it always happens the week of the second-born son's birthday and I'm so busy planning a party that I can't really juggle anything else. We know what the Age of Pinterest has done to parties, and even though I'm an underachiever when it comes to parties, I still try minimally hard.

So this year all the teachers got their thank you notes and treats a whole week late. Well. Good enough.

It seems like, at the end of every year, the kids are invited to a billion birthday parties. We receive about fifty percent of these invitations. We notice about thirty percent of the fifty percent we receive. We respond to about ten percent of the thirty percent we notice, and the boys make it out to about one percent of that ten percent.

Whatever grade you made in your statistics class, you can likely see that those are not great odds, but when you have a family with as many people in it as ours has, you have to make concessions everywhere. The five-year-old cannot go to twenty parties every year. The six-year-old cannot go to a party the same weekend his brother is involved in a chess tournament. The nine-year-old cannot go to a party that starts in two hours because he "forgot" to show us the invitation four weeks ago.

One of my sons had a missing library book at the end of this school year, and I didn't even realize it until I got this nifty little slip of paper that had the name of the book and a mug shot of my son. In large print, it said, "Book still missing from the library. Please return." So we did, and the boy didn't have to go to jail today for the crime of keeping *Creepy Carrots* here at home.

Since last September, I've been getting annoying calls from the school district cafeteria office, because on the same day, two of my boys decided to charge their lunch, even though they had a perfectly good lunch packed and ready for them. Another day, the third boy decided the cafeteria pizza looked better than his PB&J, so he joined his brothers with a lunch charge. And because schools don't make it easy to pay for school lunches anymore, unless you have an online code that we lost way back on the second day of school, they've been calling three times a day (one for each boy) since the fifth week of school. I have three hundred forty-three messages from the cafeteria office on my phone. If you call me and my mailbox is full, that's why.

They even called on Christmas. That's dedication.

The boys' wardrobe has gone seriously downhill, because, honestly, we've stopped caring. On the first day of school, my kids were dressed like the cool, clean boys they are. Now they wear sweat shorts with soccer socks pulled up to their knees, along with the dirtiest-looking shirt they could find in their closet. The oldest, this morning, stepped out of the house with both his knees flapping through his sweat pants and his ankles showing because he grew three inches over the course of this school year. It's not important. School's almost out, and they'll probably just stay in their pajamas all summer. Or, better yet, their underwear. It'll save me a few loads of laundry every week.

Related to this wardrobe decline is the deteriorating state of their shoes. These poor shoes are only hanging by a thread (I know how you feel, shoes). The problem is, my boys are required to wear tennis shoes for their physical education class. And here at the end of the year, I don't want to buy *new* tennis shoes, because summers in Texas cannot be borne in anything but flip flops. So if we buy them new tennis shoes here at the end of the school year, they won't get worn. And by the time my sons start school in the fall, their feet will have grown three sizes. I'll save my cash, thanks. Son number two can walk with flapping soles, for all I care.

The end of every school year cannot be mentioned without this failure: an increased number of tardies. I used to care about my boys being late to school, but, honestly, we're all a little tired of trying to get to school by 7:40 a.m. When someone didn't even climb out of bed until 7:15 because he stayed up too late eating the frozen pancakes I put in the freezer so they'd have breakfast this morning, there's no point in really trying. It's gonna be a late day.

When I was in eighth grade, I ran track and won the district gold medal in the four-hundred-meter dash. The first track meet of my freshman year of high school, my track coach thought it would be a good idea to put me, who was only used to running the four-hundred-meter dash, in the eight-hundred-meter run. This is not a dash, it's a run.

I ran it like a dash.

I started out the race in first place. I finished the first lap with all the other runners two hundred meters behind me, and then I remembered I still had another lap. And then, because I still had another lap and my legs had already turned into floppy limbs made of pudding that I couldn't feel anymore, all those runners passed me.

My pride was so wounded by that appalling race that I crossed the finish line with the biggest, most sheepish smile I could muster. When my coach angrily strode over to me, she said, "If I ever see you cross another finish line like a beauty queen, I'm going to put you in the mile."

Well, personally, I don't think there's anything wrong with finishing a race dead last and looking like a beauty queen.

So I'm finishing this school year strong, with a sparkling smile and a wave.

THINGS THAT MAKE YOU THROW UP YOUR HANDS

Kids and Their Ears: a Study in Irony

The other day we were driving in our van, and the boys wanted us to turn on the radio, which they tried to communicate by asking twelve times, in quick succession, "May we please listen to the radio?" We didn't even have time to answer before the next one would ask in the exact same way, not even varying the words or tone. It was somewhat alarming.

In a house with so many, I'm regularly astonished by things like this.

The problem with turning on the radio when we're in the car is that as soon as the music begins blaring into the backseat (Husband and I adjust the direction of the radio so we can talk in the front—cars are the best places to talk, because all the kids are strapped in with nowhere to go. Although sometimes that can also work against you.) the nine-year-old suddenly remembers that he has five billion words to say. He will accomplish this spectacle of word-vomiting, or attempt to accomplish it, by yelling his thoughts and random observations over the din of the music. Which then makes his brothers yell, "Be quiet! I'm trying to listen to music!" in some nice and not-so-nice ways so that Husband and I then have to address issues of honor and respect with a diatribe on how brothers are forever friends, after which everyone in the car says, "What?" because the music is still on and nobody heard a word.

Husband will turn off the radio and say, "Speak in an honoring way to each other." And then he'll turn it back on, eliminating the possibility of counter arguments.

One of the most interesting things about my children is this contrast between what they don't hear and what they do.

The other day we were, again, driving in the van with the radio blasting, and we'd just told (or shouted to) our nine-year-old to stop hitting his brother, and he said, "What?" three times. We turned off the radio and told him, for the fourth time, to stop hitting his brother, and then we turned the radio back on. The volume of the music was exactly the same as it had been. Husband, in a normal speaking voice, mentioned his name—to me, not to him—and he heard everything that was said after the mention of his name. He even repeated it back to us, word for word.

Tell me how this can be possible.

My sons can't hear me say that they must have all the LEGO pieces cleaned up by the time the timer goes off or the LEGOs will be in the sad, secret space of exiled toys. They can't hear me calling their name when they're playing outside and now it's time to come back in and take a bath, because they're having so much fun that the fun blocks out the sound of my voice. They can't hear me announce that it's cleanup time;

they'll just act like they don't know what cleanup time is and go right on playing with the cars and building a new track and making a bigger and more out-of-control mess.

They can't hear me say it's now no longer time to play with Pokémon cards and will go ballistic when those Pokémon cards get confiscated. They can't hear me call their name a thousand times to get their attention because I have something important to tell them or I need to relay some instructions. They can't hear me when I ask them did they hear me.

They can't hear me when I tell them to stop pummeling each other for the red LEGO piece, when there are five hundred other red LEGO pieces just like this one. They don't hear me when I say I've had just about enough. They don't hear me when they're playing at the table and I tell them it would be wise to stop because they're going to spill something, and then they do. And it's usually milk. All over the wall, themselves, and the floor.

They can't hear me when I instruct them to set the table or do their after-dinner chores or toss their clothes in the laundry basket or remember to put their shoes where they belong or any of the other billions of nagging instructions I have to give them every other minute of every day.

Basically, they won't really hear anything I have to say if it (a) contains more than three words and (b) doesn't contain the preamble of repeating their name at least three times and (c) doesn't interest them in the least. (For those who are quick, you already know: the only thing they hear is their name. Everything after is disqualified, unless it's something they're not supposed to hear.)

We work hard on our communication in my home. Communication is the foundation for healthy relationships. My boys have a hearing problem, which we've tried to point out. But they don't hear us.

The things they do hear, however, are a study in irony.

They hear the crackle of a chip bag that Husband opened in the pantry, where I'm supposed to meet him in thirty seconds. They hear us whisper something about the chocolate we're going to get later, a confession that begs a reply like, "Aren't you supposed to be eating better?" They hear us talking in soft murmurs about how worried we are about their uncle, and then we'll have to explain why (kids can't leave anything resting in mystery).

They'll hear our feet going down the stairs to retrieve the treats we stashed in the topmost corner of the laundry room, where they'd never be able to find them (because they're really, really bad at looking).

So I know that their inability to hear us when it's important is not a case of whether they can actually hear or not. They just, like every other kid, have selective hearing. They hear what they want. They filter out the rest.

Sometimes I wish I could do the same. Then I would live in a world that had no whining, no complaining, and no ignorance.

When you're a parent, however, this "editing" can be incredibly annoying. I can't even mention in a phone call to my mom from the privacy of my room how proud I am of one of them without the kid saying, "Are you talking about me?" He's not even home right now.

But when I tell them it's time for bed so they can get enough sleep for the Family Fun Day tomorrow that we most definitely don't want to make a Family Fight Day?

No one hears a word.

12 Reasons Parents Deserve a Participatory Award

When I was a girl in elementary school, everybody who participated in the elementary school track meet, no matter how badly they had performed, would receive a little purple participation ribbon that would, if you were me, go promptly into the trash, because all it said, to me, was "Congratulations for coming in dead last." (I would improve in middle school, thankfully. I'd even win the district championship for the four-hundred-meter dash. You wouldn't know it now, but it's my claim to fame.)

Those participation ribbons were so offensive to me, even as a kid, that purple almost stopped being my favorite color. I can't say I was a completely rational kid.

Today, if our kids come in dead last, they get trophies. That's a whole step up from a little purple participation ribbon, and it makes everybody feel like a winner.

Everybody should always feel like a winner, no trophies required.

But I get it. It's not easy to feel like a winner when another team scored its twenty-fifth run on you and your team only has a big fat zero runs. We don't want to damage our children with "better" or "best." Honestly, I'm not all that keen on competition anyway. I think it's more important that someone plays to the limit of their skill and talent, not that someone plays better than someone else.

However. As a parent, I wish all parents got awards, no matter how poorly or well they executed their parenting. I'd like a trophy that says, "World's Best Mother" even if it's just a participatory one, because then I could pretend that I actually deserved it once in a while (we're so hard on ourselves, aren't we?).

There are a whole lot of reasons that parents deserve awards. Here are some of them:

I got out of bed this morning.

Maybe you don't realize it, but this is saying a lot. I could have stayed in bed and gotten a little more sleep, but, instead, I dragged myself out, put on my running shoes (which are mandatory when you're the mom of six boys), and began the marathon that is my current reality—signing school folders, laying out lunch supplies, getting breakfast on the table and, mostly, listening to a variety of complaints—I don't like this breakfast, I need more sleep, I feel sick, I wish someone else would do this for me, on and on and on it goes.

My complaints were, by far, the loudest.

My kids have two shoes on.

Let's not talk about whether those shoes are matching shoes or a random pairing. If you're a parent, you know that kind of thing doesn't matter—one of the kid's nice tennis shoes is likely out by the trampoline, while the other is in here, right next to his Converse sneaker. Well, you're not picky. One tennis shoe, one Converse sneaker it is.

Someone seems to have played a cruel joke in our house and stolen every single right shoe my six-year-old owns. He only has two left shoes, and sometimes, when he *does* happen to stumble upon another right shoe, the left shoe is then missing. So he'll pair the recovered right shoe with a different left shoe—usually, in his case, a tennis shoe paired with a flip flop. I DON'T CARE. They're shoes. Let's go.

He'll still get half credit in his P.E. class for participating with the right half of his body. Good enough.

My kids are wearing underwear.

You would be surprised (and maybe a little disgusted) to know how many times I have to ask them about this. If you're the mom of a boy, you likely understand.

The boys in my house like to do things with their underwear other than the purpose for which underwear were created. For example, sometimes they'll use the underwear for a slingshot competition. Whoever shoots the underwear the farthest wins. Sometimes they use their boxers the way I once used a hula hoop—spinning it on their fingers, rotating it on their ankles while the other foot jumps over it. Sometimes they'll arrange every pair of skivvies they own on their head—and I can't say for sure whether they took them from their drawers or the dirty laundry pile.

The biggest problem with kids wearing underwear is *finding* underwear. Come laundry day, an entire load is spent on underwear and boxers.

When my son forgot his homework, I didn't drop it off at school for him.

There is one kid in my house who always remembers to do his homework but rarely remembers to actually turn it in. He will put the homework sheet down somewhere and not be able to remember where he left it. When I find it and hand it to him, saying, "Please put it in your backpack now," I will find it, again, in the chair where he was sitting, after everyone's safely delivered at school.

I choose not to bring him his homework, because not only is it somewhat inconvenient to pack up, again, the three kids who don't currently attend school and go back, but also he needs to learn his lesson. That tactic, however, is not working. He doesn't care about his grades—which hover in the Bs but could be higher—as much as I do.

I fed them.

If I am burning from the inside out with a vicious flu virus, I still have to feed my children. If I fall down my stairs and break my foot, I still have to feed my children. If I fall asleep on the couch until it's too late to cook dinner, I still have to feed my children.

There is always dinner. And breakfast and lunch and snacks. My entire life is feeding my children. That alone makes this worthy of an award.

My kids are sleeping.

Sure, it took me an hour to wrestle them into bed, but then all I had to do was break up that melatonin tablet into equal pieces and dole it out to them, and they're suddenly, miraculously asleep.

I'm just kidding. We only use the melatonin for the difficult children.

My kid said he hated me and I didn't say what was really on my mind.

It was dangerously close to my tongue, but over these years of being a parent, I've really learned some self-control. Instead of saying that sometimes I don't really like him, either, I kept my mouth shut, shrugged my shoulders, and thanked him for his honesty. And then I holed myself away in the pantry and ate that pan of brownies I made yesterday, because my kid hates me and there is no self-control for this.

My kid said we're the worst family ever—no other parent has rules about tech time or makes kids do chores—and I didn't laugh out loud.

I'm sure you'll agree that this was a feat worthy of a trophy.

I didn't lose it when I told my sons to stop sword fighting with the broom and they broke a light instead.

It took some heavy meditative breathing in that moment, but this is a true story. Trophy-worthy.

I successfully won an argument with a four-year-old.

It's taken years of practice, but it finally happened. Here's how it went down:

Him: The sky is yellow today.

Me: Um, no, that sky is blue.

Him: No, yellow.

Me: Looks like we're going to have to go back over our

colors, aren't we?

Him: Look, it's yellow.

He pointed toward the sky that was very clearly blue. I asked him if he had yellow sunglasses on. He smiled and said, "Yes." I pretended to take them off. He said, "Oh, yeah, the sky is blue."

I'm sure it will never happen again, but I felt like I'd accomplished something really revolutionary.

I remembered what day it was (or anything, really).

If you've been a parent for long, you know just how completely kids will steal your brain before you've even had time to appreciate its virtues. My brain usually feels like a lost cause, but today I remembered what day it was. It happened to be one of my sons' birthdays, but still. I'll be baking some cupcakes later to drop off at school, because remembering (in this case, the day) always comes at the price of forgetting something else (in this case, his birthday). But, well, it's a start.

The day is done, and I am still standing (or lying down on my bed, because my body feels like it's been run over by a truck).

Now I will likely fall asleep in a matter of seconds (but not before I receive my trophy, which you'll just have to tuck in beside me, because I can't move), and I will be able to start this dance all over again tomorrow. I'll deserve another trophy, because I'll get out of bed.

Maybe.

One Day You'll Miss It: an Undeniable Reality

People always tell you, when you're the parent of young children, that one day you're gonna miss this. It's so true. I am often bombarded with the bittersweet feeling of pride mixed with sadness when one of my sons learns to do something on his own—like pour his own glass of milk, tie his shoes, take a shower by himself.

It hollows me out a little inside.

But there are also days that have many many moments of won't-miss-this activity, days when I reach the end of my rope, days when I grit through clenched teeth: "Nope. I'm not gonna miss this at all."

I won't miss the morning they figured out how to open a lock on the front door with a magnet while I was indisposed on the toilet upstairs, and the only evidence I had of this remarkable feat was the magnet lying on the floor and the slam that shook the house on its foundation. I won't miss the mad rush outside, during which I pulled a muscle tripping across my threshold. I won't miss hauling the escape artist back inside while he yelled out to everyone who was willing to listen (or who was awake so early): "You're the worst mom in the whole world" or something equivalent to it.

I won't miss the morning they decided they wanted to make a time capsule to bury in the backyard and for the next hour they roamed around the house looking for what they could put in it.

("Your sewing scissors?"

"No."

"How about one of my shirts, so I'll remember how small I was?"

"No."

"What about one of your pieces of chocolate candy?"

"You're not supposed to know about that, first of all, and second of all, I am not letting the creatures of the earth get my chocolate."

"I would eat it before they did."

"Exactly. Creatures of the earth. Why don't you bury something of yours?"

"Because I can't be without it for five years.")

I won't miss the days they played with the plunger again, even though I've told them a billion times to leave it alone. Leave it alone. Leave it alone.

I won't miss when they called my name in rapid-fire succession, before I could even take a breath to answer, over and over again, so often I would like to change my name. Or when they tried to have a conversation with me even after I'd begun a very important discussion with Husband and they didn't care, they just kept talking over us. Or when they thought they were the only ones with something important to say.

I won't miss the afternoons they whined about being so hungry they're about to die, and then, when I put the yummy dinner on the table, they whined about how they don't even like this, and now they're REALLY going to starve because we never make any food that they like, why can't we make food they like?

I won't miss the nights they got out of bed a hundred times, especially when they came and knocked on our door and I was right in the middle of the deepest and most blissful sleep I'd ever experienced, only to be startled out of bed in a burst of heartbeat, shrieking, and a loud, thumping fall, because my reflexes are always trained for flight (a gift of anxiety). Or the nights when they stood beside my bed until my intuition sensed that something was amiss in my bedroom, and I peeled my eyes open to see a kid's face looming near mine. I won't miss the muscles I've strained getting out of bed before a night walker can get me.

I won't miss the days when they destroyed my nice pile of folded laundry ten minutes after I finished sorting. I won't miss the weeks they uncleaned my house one room at a time. I won't miss the afternoons they broke the couch or put another hole in the wall or touched the doorknob with sticky syrup hands so the next time I touched it and tried to take back my hand, half my skin peeled off.

Maybe I'll miss "this" when they no longer come to my room to tell me goodnight a million times because they're too busy talking to friends on the phone about what they did in school today and the latest social media message someone posted or whatever it is that kids talk about these days.

Maybe I'll miss "this" when they no longer sit in my lap for stories and snuggle into that place on my collarbone because they're too big for laps.

Maybe I'll miss "this" when they're no longer playing Uno with me because it's not exactly cool to play any kind of game with your parents—especially your mom.

Maybe I'll miss "this" when playing dodgeball parents-against-kids actually starts to hurt.

Maybe I'll miss "this" when they ask not to have dinner with us but with a friend—or, worse, a girlfriend (the answer's always no, sons).

Maybe I'll miss "this" when they close up their mouth and we have to pry it open to hear obligatory answers like "yes" and "no," while we're waiting for more that never comes.

Maybe I'll miss "this" when they no longer have to be reminded to put on their deodorant so they don't scare everybody off.

Maybe I'll miss "this" when their rooms stay clean because they're never home anymore.

Oh, who am I kidding? I'm going to miss it all.

A neighbor just texted me. She saw one of my boys running down the street—in his underwear.

And you know what? I'll even miss this.

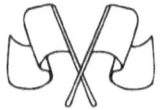

Things Kids Do Before Leaving the House: an Inventory

It takes my family the longest time to get out the door when we're trying to leave.

One of the reasons for this is that my kids are really bad at packing up the billion things they want to take wherever we're going. Many of these things are unnecessary, in my opinion. I mean, I guess you never know when you're going to need that LEGO mini figure to strike up a conversation with a potential friend—but could you just take one or two, instead of forty? One of them is probably going to get lost (every single time), and then you'll have to live with regret you could have avoided.

My kids will pack up toy dinosaurs, crayons, notebooks, books. These last two I understand; I take three of each myself. ("Can't you just take one?" Husband says when he's digging for a diaper that's been smashed down to the bottom of my backpack. I shrug. "I never know which one I'll want to read or write in," I say.)

The biggest part of this equation, though, is all the things kids *do* before leaving that parents don't even think about.

They'll grab all the change they can find in the house,

because we might be going to a store, and we don't know where their wallets are. They'll spend an hour flipping over every cushion in our house to search for spare change—even though Husband and I very rarely carry cash or coins.

They'll change their underwear. It is such a mystery why this one makes the list, even though I've had plenty of time to contemplate it. (I've been sitting here, staring at the words for the last half-hour, trying to make sense of them. There is no sense to be made.) They say they want to have fresh underwear. Well, that underwear was fresh last night when you put it on. What usually follows is a sheepish shrug and a half-grin. Go on, then.

They'll change their clothes. I don't know why they need to change their clothes to go to the zoo, especially since they changed from shorts to jeans, and it's a three-digit day. But whatever. They'll be wishing they'd stayed in their breezy workout shorts instead of donning skinny jeans and a black top hat to look a little cool (he's only seven. I think we're in for some interesting teenage years.).

They'll purposely find mismatching shoes, because everybody knows that one tennis shoe and one flip flop is the best way to walk around the Alamo in downtown San Antonio. Also, it's cool. And they like making other people think they don't have parents, because maybe someone who's much nicer than their mom and dad—and by much nicer, they mean lets them watch television and play video games all day every day —will offer to take them home. Then they'll never have to do chores again (to live in the delusional mind of a child, I think, would be blissful sometimes).

They'll grab their stuffed animal buddy, because they don't want him to be lonely at the house. I will usually gently point out that he's not a real dog. He is, though, the boy will insist. And then the boy will leave his stuffed animal buddy in the hot car so he can suffocate while we're out and about. I gently point this out, too. The boy usually says, "He's not a real dog, Mama." So I'm confused. Which is the perpetual state of a parent.

They'll make a massive mess of the art cabinet looking for some crayons to take along with them in their backpack—for the art that might strike them at the most unpredictable of times. Likely, just because they packed it with crayons, they will forget this backpack in the car, so excited are they to race into the children's museum. These crayons will melt all over the books they shoved inside the same backpack. Which were also library books.

They'll pack a book or five. This isn't a problem; I bring books everywhere, too. The real problem comes when we're out in a museum, and they've brought that backpack holding five books with them—in case they get bored—and now they're complaining that it's too heavy to carry, could we carry it for them?

Nope.

They'll eat some toothpaste real quick. It's much quicker than brushing their teeth, and more efficient, too—your throat and tongue and everything now smell like Wicked Cool Mint. Bad breath solved in one little swallow.

They'll pack some chocolate in their back pocket when

we're not looking. I don't even know where they got the chocolate, but they found some. Without asking, they shoved it into their pocket, to be found by yours truly later, when it's all melted to look like something else is coming out the back of the pants.

They'll air condition the world of Central Texas by leaving the door wide open, hastily retreating after we told them, for the thousandth time, to get in the car.

They'll run a few laps around the cul-de-sac, no matter if they're in church clothes or something more casual. They want to get their energy out before they're strapped in the car. Me? I already lost all my energy in the effort of herding six kids out the door.

Sometimes I really don't understand my kids. All the things they think to do before they even leave the house is astounding. I just grab my purse and hope everything's in it. Which usually isn't the case; the last time I took them all to the grocery store, I used this method (I should have learned by now) and had to turn around and come back home to retrieve my wallet. And by the time I got back home, I didn't have enough stamina to take them to the grocery store.

We just ate raisins and bread that night. I told them we were pretending we lived in the times before there were big grocery stores. They believed me.

One of these days we'll get really good at leaving. Boys will shuffle to the car with only the clothes on their backs. Or there won't be any more boys to shuffle to the car, because they'll be grown and gone.

And then, I think, I'll miss the days when it felt like a production just to get out the door.

So today, when it's time to pack up and take a trip to the library, I watch the madness with a smile on my face. I can't change their quirks—but I can certainly enjoy them.

And I do.

Pokémon: A Wandering Admission

The other day I was walking through the grocery store, minding my own business, happy to finally take a trip without my kids, when I saw a boy who was talking nonstop to his mother. I recognized the sort of boy he was, because I have a son just like him, and while I love talking to children, I was in a hurry.

I tried to sneak on by.

He, of course, immediately spotted me and said hello. (I have a friendly face. What can I say?)

I smiled politely and said hello back.

"Do you play Pokémon Go?" he said, holding up a phone that was likely his mother's.

"No," I said, laughing just a little bit uncomfortably. My boys collect Pokémon cards, but they don't play the game on devices.

"You really should," he said. "The store is full of them."

He went on and on, telling me about how many he'd caught already, and I could feel the time leaking away in a giant suck of air while his mother stood by looking at me helplessly. She seemed to be saying, *Please. Make it stop.*

I smiled at her with mutual understanding.

When I was in high school, my stepbrother, who was in middle school, had a Pokémon obsession. I didn't like them then, and I don't like them now that my boys are interested in them.

Maybe I've just never given them a chance. But it's hard to give them a chance when the thing they seem to be most made for is a trading card carpet in my house.

We have a place for Pokémon cards. They never end up in that place.

I don't have as much of an aversion to Pokémon Go as the actual physical cards, other than the fact that I think it's a fad. (And, as of the publishing of this book, it appears that's exactly what it was. Who has heard of Pokémon Go now?)

Two days after that grocery store visit, when Husband and I took our boys to the local library for our weekly visit, we saw some people venturing up to the building, ducking behind it, and then walking around as though they were lost. We thought maybe it was their first time visiting and they didn't know where the entrance was. Husband politely called, "The doors are right over there" and pointed. They pretended not to hear him. One of them finally called out, "I got it!"

We realized they were playing Pokémon Go.

Two other groups filtered through before a dad and his kid walked to the same side of the library and wandered around like they were lost. At this point, I looked at Husband and Husband looked at me, and we both said without saying, "Oh my goodness."

We burst out laughing.

I'm really not trying to poke fun (which is just two letters and a space away from Pokémon, if you haven't noticed) at anyone who plays the game. If this is the way you get your exercise, do it. If it brings you joy, do it. If you cannot imagine your life without Pokémon Go, please, live your life with it.

I only bring up Pokémon Go to say that my observations have led me to believe that I have a grand idea for another, similar game. I set my twins loose, you round them up.

They would love it. They are the wanderers of my family. Every time we go somewhere public, they disappear for a minimum of ten minutes while we all try not to panic. (Their daddy and I are the only ones who panic, actually. Their brothers think it's funny. "You lost them again?" they say.) This is why we need a tracking device—a game that will make rounding up our twins easier.

You don't have to tell me that this idea won't work. It's not a virtual game, it's a realistic one, and no one wants to play that. And if I only offered it virtually, it wouldn't give me the break I need from my terrorizing two.

I will say that the Pokémon cards have offered my boys and me some good bonding time. They like to play the card game, and even though I don't understand the rules, because they change depending on who's playing (I'm usually the loser. I think it's just a coincidence, though.), I typically spend our playing time memorizing the way his eyebrows arch over his eyes or the perfect ovals of his fingernails or the chin that is no longer soft but is becoming a young man's.

In this way, Pokémon enhances my life.

Before I left the grocery store where the kid asked me if I played Pokémon Go, I actually, honestly, wished that I did and that was exactly why I'd come to the store in the first place: to round up Pokémon.

Have you ever seen the kind of grocery budget it takes to feed six boys?

Why Does My Towel Smell Like Butt?

The other day I was enjoying the rare privilege of a shower, and as soon as I got out to dry off, I noticed a smell emanating from my towel. It smelled of something feral and gross… something like…butt.

Why would my towel smell like butt? I don't do anything to it that would make it smell like butt.

The mystery didn't seem all that important to me, though, so I simply got a new towel, in the process dripping water all over the floor like I used to do as a kid. I never cleaned it up when I was a kid. I didn't clean it up as an adult, either, and my six-year-old shouted at me when he slipped and "broke his knee" (he could walk just fine) in the puddle while on his way to get a Band-Aid he didn't really need. When I explained to him that I only have so much time for a shower, which most definitely does not include the extra time it takes to find a towel that doesn't smell like butt *and* clean up the water I might have dripped in the process, he looked at me and said, "You said a bad word. You said 'butt.'"

"So did you," I pointed out. He tried to wipe off his grin. I know the game. They say the "bad" words every chance they get. Butt, fart, it never gets old.

My older boys typically bathe in our garden tub for now, because it's easier to run bath time like an assembly line: three in one bath, washed by one parent; three in the other bath, washed by the other parent. I typically read to the six- and seven-year-old while they bathe together, and the nine-year-old has the privilege of bathing by himself while I read an entirely different story.

One particular night, when the alarm chimed, telling me it was time for the oldest to get out so we could begin our family story time, I walked out of the bathroom to pick up my Silent Reading book. I walked out to our home library and saw that Husband was already reading and that I'd forgotten my timer. So I re-entered my bathroom, where the nine-year-old had been bathing, at a time when I was not normally present.

Drying-off time.

It suddenly all made sense.

The nine-year-old had my towel in his hands. He was drying off, and when he'd finished, he rubbed it all up and down his hind parts, like he was a dog trying to scratch an itch.

"Uh, what are you doing with my towel?" I said.

"I didn't have one, so I just used the one that was hanging up," he said.

I pointed to the side of the garden tub, where a towel was draped. I had draped it there. "You didn't see that towel?"

He shook his head. "Did you just put that there?" he said, with a half smile and a suspicious eye.

"No," I said. Trust me. No. It's been there all along.

"Well, I didn't see it," he said.

"So you just thought you'd use mine," I said.

"I thought it was Daddy's," he said.

The mystery has been solved: the nine-year-old has been using my towel. And not just using my towel but abusing it. And the only reason he reached for it is because it was the only one hanging up.

I guess that's a good reason for leaving your towel on the floor, Husband.

That's where mine's going from here on out.

On Permanent Markers and Kids: a Horrifying Examination

The other day, for a Family Time activity, I took out some brand new permanent markers so my boys and Husband and I could do some blackout poetry together. I would teach them how, they would be responsible permanent marker users, and we would have some art at the end of our time together.

The eyes of my twins, who are four, lit up. "Permanent markers!" they said, so excited they could barely contain it.

"Well, not for you," I said, because I know what permanent markers mean in the hands of four-year-olds. I've raised three other four-year-olds. "I have regular markers for you."

We had a grand time marking out words and creating our own poetry from the pages of some of my books. And when we were finished, I packed up those permanent markers, to shove in a secret drawer in my room.

I'm no fool. I know what kids can and will do with permanent markers. Things that include:

Draw a mustache on Daddy's face while he's sleeping.

The six-year-old thought of this one; he never carried it out because Daddy never slept in his presence. So he drew it on himself instead. The day before school picture day.

Transform your face into a lion's face.

I'll never forget the time I had to email my third son's kindergarten teacher and explain that the green marks on his face were sustained by a permanent marker. Yes, he'd had a bath, but permanent markers take a while to fade. "He'll be at school looking like a lion for several days," I warned.

I'm sure she laughed hard about it when she saw him. He was an impressive green lion.

Turn your solid yellow shirt into a bumblebee shirt.

The day I caught my second son doing this, he said, "I like yellow and black stripes better than plain yellow."

Well, that's a good thing, because permanent markers are permanent.

We still have that shirt; it's been through three other boys so far. It has been beloved by every one of them—crooked stripes and all.

Make hieroglyphics on the wall and say it wasn't you.

Write your name on your brother's backpack and say it wasn't you.

Draw a treasure map on your bed sheet and say it wasn't you.

You'll notice a pattern here. There was a time, in our very recent history, when one of our twins had a permanent marker secretly stashed somewhere. We searched every crevice in his room. We suspect that he possesses the disturbing ability to swallow things without digesting them so he can then cough them back up at will. He usually performed this yet-unproven trick after we closed his door for nap time.

He drew on walls, doors, and sheets. The only plan he had for consequence-aversion was to say it wasn't him, even though his twin brother, who shared the room with him and had the good sense to stay out of his moments of blissful delinquency, could corroborate the facts.

"It was him," his twin would say.

As if I needed more proof than the name he signed on every masterpiece.

A permanent marker, we discovered, could also be used for coloring more black keys on the piano—an act that had multiple reasons, according to the logic of a five-year-old: (1) he needed to remember where middle C was (he colored the wrong key) and (2) he wanted more flats and sharps on the keyboard (because coloring the keys makes it so). That fiasco introduced us to the magic of a dry erase marker: you color over permanent marker (on some surfaces) with a dry erase marker, and the permanent marker disappears.

My boys have, over the years, used permanent markers to outline their faces on the bathroom mirror in a portrait they thought would last forever. They've used them to color their shoes black. They've used them to provide their own illustrations in their mom's favorite picture book (the snail on the last page has, collectively, drawn the most laughs during re-reads).

They've given themselves black highlights, drawn their own temporary tattoos, and, best of all, once labeled their identical twin baby brothers so they could tell them apart.

Husband didn't wash the twins' foreheads for weeks, because, even though he wouldn't admit this, he used the labels, too.

Permanent markers were put away for a while in our house, for obvious reasons. But I thought, since the boys have gotten older, it might be fun to bring them back out—for art purposes and only when supervised. I collect them all at the end of our art sessions and hide them away in a secret place where kids will never find them (right next to my stash of chocolate mints).

Problem is, I just counted my supply—and we're missing one.

BOYS?!!

The Seven Articles in a Brother Bill of Rights

My boys spend a lot of time together.

Part of this is intentional, because Husband and I require family time. It's good for the family. Part of it, though, is unintentional and has to do with the arrangements of our house.

We have a smallish house, so we have three boys crammed together in one bedroom and three crammed into another. There's not much space for a boy to call his own, unless you're talking about closets and the undersides of beds.

Because they spend so much time in each others company, I have been able to observe that my sons operate by a sibling bill of rights that look something like this:

Article 1: If you find it, you get to keep it.

It doesn't matter if it's a pair of missing underwear three sizes too small that hasn't been washed in a very long time. Finders, keepers. It could be a penny they found, which is worth almost nothing; a toy someone forget to pick up that has no value whatsoever because it's missing its left arm; an old petrified carrot remnant from an undetermined time in the past.

Everything is fair game.

Article 2: If you hit, I get to hit back.

My boys get in slap fights several times a day. If you come by my house between the hours of 6 a.m. and 8:30 p.m. (which is when my kids are awake), you're most likely to hear, within minutes, the symphony of slaps that result in yells, wails, and even bigger slaps.

Some days I just let them duke it out, because they'll be laughing about something a few minutes later, the best of friends again.

Article 3: If you're strong enough to take it, it's yours, of course.

We have a lot of parameters and boundaries in our family. We don't allow bullying or diminishing or taking things from the hands of anyone else. In fact, in this area, we have a mantra: "Use your words, and if your words don't work, ask for help." Our sons are advised (endlessly, it seems) to use this mantra when one of their brothers has something that belongs to them and they want it back.

Do they use it? Not usually. The strongest is the winner.

My older boys aren't going to like this strongest-is-the-winner philosophy when their little brothers turn into teenagers and they're all the same size. Paybacks are hard.

Article 4: If you lose something, blame a brother.

Our oldest is the king of blaming his brothers. Any time a LEGO piece wanders away from his work station in the garage, he blames his brothers for it. Usually he'll find it, later, in his pocket. When he brought a notebook to a zoo outing the other day, he started freaking out because he couldn't find it.

"Twins!" he yelled, racing after them like he was going to give them a beat-down. (I'll give him this: they're the usual culprits.) They, of course, split and ran in opposite directions. While he was chasing one of them, the notebook dropped out from where it was tucked under his armpit.

I'm sure it'll be funny in a few days.

Article 5: If you beat others to tattling, you won't get in trouble.

My boys never work in isolation. They never hit or mimic or dish out a shove unprovoked. They are constantly in a cycle of annoy, hit, hit, annoy. And because of this, I have been near knocked over by a barreling kid who wants to tattle first.

"Mama, my brother kicked me," one of my twins will say.

What he's not saying is that he first hit his brother with a Hot Wheels truck that shouldn't even be out in the backyard.

The other day, one after another of them streamed through the back door at different times, tears wetting their cheeks and siren-like cries fraying my nerves. They each came in to tattle. And it was always the same old story: "My brother hit me in the face."

"What in the world is going on?" I said, and I marched out back with my hands on my hips.

They were playing the slapping game. I didn't even feel sorry for them. I locked the door behind me and tried to ignore the symphony of wails that waited on the deck.

Article 6: If there are twelve of the same exact toy, you

should still try to steal the one in your brother's hands.

I will never understand the logic of this phenomenon. We have a room full of LEGO pieces. We've set up our garage to be a LEGO workstation so our boys can enjoy their building and we don't have to nag them every other minute about keeping the mess contained. They're responsible for how neat or how out-of-hand their LEGO station is.

When I say we have millions of LEGO pieces, I mean we have millions of pieces. This is what happens when you have six children who are all obsessed with LEGOs. Everybody buys them LEGOs for their birthday. Multiple sets. Of the same thing—because, you know, sets don't stay together for more than a week. Or at least that's the case in my house.

It stands to reason that with so many LEGO pieces, there are going to be duplicate LEGO pieces. Maybe even hundreds of duplicates. But when one kid needs the piece another kid has in his hand, he doesn't dig in the excess pieces; he takes the one that's in his brother's hand. And then both are off and running trying to justify why the piece belongs to them. ("I'm the only one who makes teeth marks like that!" "But I scratched it right here on the side, see?")

At least they're exercising their powers of observation.

Article 7: If someone's mean to your brother and they're not part of the family, shut it down.

I love the relationship my boys have with one another. They can be pummeling each other one second, but if or when another kid from down the street steps in to take part in the pummeling, my boys will quickly draw the boundary line.

Nobody gets to mess with their brother. Except them.

I hope they always look out for each other and draw boundary lines around what their friends can say about the members of their family. I hope they always stand up for each other. I hope they always find, at the end of a day, that they are more than brothers: they are friends.

There's nobody quite like a brother.

If a Kid Wants to Do a Time Capsule

If a kid wants to do a time capsule he'll bury in your backyard, first he'll ask for a box.

When you give him a box, he'll ask for a few "simple" craft supplies so he can have something to fill it. He'll ask for some markers so he can color a bookmark "to remember how he used to get all outside the lines when he was a little boy." When he's finished coloring the bookmark, he'll ask for some memorabilia. Which means he'll need access to your stack of old "treasure" papers so he can find something interesting that will remind him of his third grade year.

When you've told him, no, we're not getting a stack of papers out, he'll ask if he can stick his brother in the time capsule instead, and you'll probably think he's joking, but then you'll notice the look he's giving his brother, sizing him up as though to see whether he'll actually fit in the box. And you'll hesitate, because his brother, right now, is running off with the scissors he knows he's not supposed to touch, with some loose strands of hair in his fist. But then, of course, you'll say no. Of course you will.

You will.

He'll then ask for a pen to write his future self a note and sign his name in the cursive he taught himself this summer. He'll take so long writing the note you'll ask him why he's writing an entire book that he'll have to sit down and read in five years, after he digs it all back up (if he remembers where he buried it, that is), and your asking him why he's *writing* a book will remind him that he wants to put an actual *already-written* book from your bookshelves into his time capsule, because of course he'll want to read a Pokémon graphic novel when he's fourteen. When you say, no, he can't put that book inside his time capsule, he'll huff a little and ask you which book he *can* put inside the time capsule, and when you tell him that he can't put any book in it because a book buried under the ground will likely begin to decompose, he'll ask you if you think food would start to decompose, because even though he's practically a genius in science, apparently he hasn't learned or read about this part of the scientific process.

When you say yes, food will decompose, he'll say, that's okay, he thinks he'll go ahead and put this whole bunch of grapes in it, and you'll explain that not only is there no point to putting a whole bunch of grapes in a time capsule, because they'll be gone in another month, but we also don't waste food around the house, and he'll have to come up with something else to put in the box. So he'll realize, now, that the cardboard box will probably actually decompose during the time he plans to keep it underground, so he'll ask for something more permanent—like a plastic container you're not using. Before you've even answered, he'll open up the cabinet where you keep all your containers, and he'll rummage through the perfectly organized stacks until he finds a small glass one and holds it up so high that if he were to drop it, glass would shatter instantaneously.

Once all that's sorted out and he's taped up his box and is ready to go, he'll ask for a shovel. You'll tell him that you saw the shovel out in the front yard, and he'll say, oh, yeah, his brother brought it out there because they were playing a sword fighting game and whoever got hit in the face and was still standing at the end of it was the king of the mountain, and you'll look at him, slack-jawed, and he'll take advantage of that moment to go out front and retrieve the shovel.

Then he'll ask you where you'd like him to dig the hole.

Naturally, you'll look around the backyard, which is already pretty much destroyed, and you'll say nowhere, because there are enough holes already, can't he just use one of the pre-dug ones? But he won't let it rest, so you'll point vaguely in a direction, knowing that it won't really make much difference anyway, but you'll add that he's going to do the digging himself. He'll look at the ground and stick the shovel in, and you'll hear a jarring clang, because the soil is mostly rock. He'll try again—and one more time—before he'll ask you to help. You'll politely decline, saying you need to get back inside to make sure his brother isn't smashing flower pots for fun like you caught him doing the other day, and he'll probably say something along the lines of no one loves him because no one will help him dig, and you'll say something like he just wants to make someone else do the heavy lifting for him, and he'll say something like you're the meanest person in the whole world, but then he'll ask you if you might actually give him a hand, please, because the ground is full of rocks, and he can't do it. And you'll feel a little sorry of him, so you'll dig a little, too, even though all you have is a hand shovel, since he's using the large one, swinging it so close to your head you hold up your hands and tell him you don't want to be king of the mountain, please put it down.

Then he'll ask how far he has to dig.

You'll tell him that he'll have to dig as far down as he needs to for the box to be buried, because you certainly don't want a cardboard box with Amazon's logo on it sticking out from the earth, and then he'll tell you that he no longer wants to do a time capsule anymore, because he wants the Pokémon card he put in it. And he also wants to start a "Minecraft ideas" business in the front yard.

So you'll both go back inside, where his brothers have taken out every card game you have in your house and spread them all over the floor to "be a new carpet because ours is really dirty and gross," and the cardboard box will wait for another day, when your kid will look at it, recognize its potential, and remember that day he wanted to do a time capsule. And chances are, if he remembers he wants to do a time capsule, he's going to want something to put in it.

The Dangers of Blinking: You Really Will Miss It

There's some age-old advice that every parent hears at one time or another: blink and you'll miss it.

It's sage advice when talking about the passage of time. I often marvel at how quickly the years pass; it seems that I've blinked a time or two, and my oldest is now nine.

What happened?

This is also sage advice when you have kids like mine—kids who take every opportunity to do what they're not supposed to do when I take a moment to "blink." (This may or may not be because sometimes "blinking" is synonymous with accidentally falling asleep for an undetermined amount of time. I'm tired.)

Here are some of the things I've missed when I've blinked:

Someone got into the dry erase markers. Or, worse, the permanent markers.

I keep markers in the art cabinet, because my boys like to color with them. I've tried to tell them that real artists don't usually use markers (at least not the Crayola kind), because markers don't allow for the proper shading techniques. They don't care. Markers are fun—especially when they get on the hands and face. They'll have laughing fits when their hands are completely green from coloring all afternoon with a marker.

Markers aren't really a problem. They're washable. The real problem is when a rogue dry erase marker or permanent marker gets closed into the marker container. I'll "blink" and then wake up with cat whiskers on my face, drawn in black permanent marker that no amount of scrubbing will take away. It's especially unfortunate that I have an author talk tomorrow.

Dry erase marker doesn't erase permanent marker on the skin, in case you were wondering. It just results in a bright pink reinforcement of the original black masterpiece.

The food is all gone.

If I blink for any amount of time or even, for a moment, let down my guard when my kids are home, they will completely raid our fridge. They have no kind of impulse control and also no shut-off button when it comes to food. They get this from Husband, who told me, before we were married, that he was once affectionately known among his friends' parents as "The Garbage Disposal." If someone didn't want to eat their food, whatever it was, Husband would finish it. If someone had extra food in their house, Husband would eat it. If there were snacks in the pantry of another person's house, Husband would eat it.

If I spent as much time blinking as I would like to spend blinking, we would have no food in our house the day after grocery day. Which might, now that I think about it, be better for my figure.

Maybe I'll schedule a blink session this afternoon.

The walls become murals.

We have a plan, when our boys are older, to turn most of the walls in our house into murals. I don't know if we'll actually do this; it's been on the list of things to do for a long time. But there's a reason that we'd save this for later—and it's mostly because the majority of our boys (the oldest three excepted) are not very good at drawing. Yet. They draw people like they are oversized heads with legs coming directly from their chins. And this doesn't make for the best kind of mural.

If I blink, we will end up with cave drawings all over the walls. I know, because this happened once when my twins were supposed to be sleeping. I woke to delightful hieroglyphics scribbled onto the walls by two-year-olds. At least they had the foresight to do it with chalk, which they then spent the rest of the afternoon washing off. Natural consequences and all.

They, of course, got better with practice. They've now succeeded in coloring a door red, writing something illegible (illegible only because they're four) on the wall behind their bed, and finishing a crayon mural inside their closet.

All the silverware ends up outside.

I once sat down in a chair, intending to look over a few notes, and promptly blinked. I woke to an empty silverware drawer. I saw my boys outside, sword fighting with butterknives, using spoons as shields, and wearing forks in their hair. Our cloth napkins were tied around their foreheads, like bands. It was like a scene from *Lord of the Flies* or something.

The other day Husband had our boys clean up the

backyard because he was going to do one of his twice-a-year mowing sessions. It was amazing all the stuff they brought in. I didn't think we had that many kitchen things. They found fifteen spoons (they've been sharing spoons on their "Cereal Saturdays"), twenty-one forks (they use serving forks to eat), and thirty-three cups (they've been drinking from bowls).

I feel like a proper chef now. Except for my cooking skills. But at least I can set an impressive table.

Tech time becomes all the time.

Husband and I are stubbornly strict about the amount of technology time, which we "affectionately" call Brain Rot Time, our kids get. We're both creative people who would much rather our kids be reading or drawing or writing in journals or playing outside.

But if we blinked for a certain number of minutes, our kids would, in no time, locate all the devices in our house (which we try to hide like the mean parents we are) and play on them forever and ever and ever. Our oldest has, in fact, gotten in trouble a few times because he's snuck some technology devices out of hiding places at night and stayed up most of the night watching YouTube videos. We got better hiding places after that—which is to say, all the technology devices now sit in a box underneath our bed, turned off. If they were (a) taken from the box, our Parent Sense would kick in (if the jolt to the bed didn't wake us) and (b) turned on, they'd announce themselves in a flourish of chimes.

Now we can blink peacefully.

The house would become a national disaster area.

Hills I'll Probably Lie Down On

If you've ever tried to mobilize kids for a good old-fashioned cleaning session, you know what I'm talking about. Kids have an inborn aversion to cleaning up after themselves. Our boys are required to tidy up the house every day before they have their tech time; we've tried to explain to them that if they just cleaned up after themselves in the first place, this wouldn't be such a time-consuming problem for them, but the lesson has yet to connect with their brains. They drag their feet around, looking at all the coloring books and crayons and books and capes and swords and board games and cards they got out and didn't put back away, moaning about how this will take forever and they'll never get their tech time.

Imagine if Husband and I weren't around—because we were blinking—to enforce this requirement. The house would continue to accumulate its mess—the second law of thermodynamics, otherwise known as entropy, works especially well in a home with children—and boys would likely not feel the need to lift a finger until something important (like, perhaps, a technological device) got lost.

Not the least of the disaster-area rooms would be the kitchen. Not only would there be thirty-three cups (rescued from the Great Outdoors) sitting by the sink for the seven people (I have a Klean Kanteen and rarely use a cup) in the house who use them, but there would also be dangerous puddles of melted ice on the floor because my boys are obsessed with ice in cups (hey, they say it's a good snack, so I try not to complain). They drop these cubes and don't tell anyone. Entering the kitchen when my sons are home is an every-day challenge of Staying On Your Feet.

A house that has been blinked in would have books all over the floor. And notebooks left where boys finished writing in them. And shoes left where they took them off. And…

Well, this list could go on forever.

The other day I was resting on the couch, reading a book, and I decided I needed to blink for a minute. I guess it was for longer than a minute, though, because when I woke up, the Christmas tree was turned over on its side, the magazines were spilled out all over the floor, and the creepy Elf on the Shelf was staring right in my eyes—and we don't even have an Elf on the Shelf.

My kids blamed the cat.

I guess I'll never know. That's the sort of thing you miss when you blink.

WHAT IT LOOKS LIKE ON TOP OF THE HILL

The Diary of a Mom Eater: a Horror Story

I've decided to eat healthy again.

We've just had a long week and weekend of rewarding ourselves for getting through the day. It was more than that, actually. It's incredibly counter-productive to have a birthday at the end of January, right during the time you've hit your stride with healthier living. You start off the new year on fantastic footing, getting your eating under control after the holidays, and then you're bombarded with a birthday and the irresistible temptation to relax your food rules a little—take a day or maybe two days or maybe the whole week.

You can see how this quickly becomes a snowball.

I don't know why I haven't thought of it before, but this yearly struggle could likely be alleviated by starting my new year in February. And pretending Valentine's Day doesn't exist.

So here we are, a week past my birthday. I'm ready. Let's do this.

No sugar for the next thirty days. A cleanse. My favorite thing to do.

Sunday night

I'll start tomorrow. Tonight I'll eat an entire container of Ben & Jerry's delectable ice cream in my favorite flavor: "The Tonight Dough."

Monday early early morning

The day unfolds like it's stacked against me: with (surprise and oh, joy!) my monthly visitor. But I am strong. I can do this.

Monday early morning

Workout's finished, it's time to get the boys up for school. I can totally do this. Totally.

We race out the door, to walk the school boys to their elementary school three blocks down the road. My four-year-old twins don't wait to cross the street, because they think, erroneously, that they're competent at everything. They almost get run over. Now they have to hold on to the stroller, so they're both wailing. One is refusing to move forward, so he gets to be carried. He weighs a lot. I already did my workout for the day, and now here's another.

I deserve a reward. I resist.

We're home. I let the twins race for the front door. They get there before me, which means they have an opportunity to do something real quick before I push inside with the stroller carrying their baby brother. The something they do is grab the markers their second-oldest brother left out this morning and color the piece of art he was drawing for me, which he was planning to finish after he got home from school. When I walk in, the one doing the coloring, which he should know, by now, he's not supposed to be doing, after countless lectures about coloring on other people's art, says, "My brother left this for me to color." The picture is ruined, and not just a little bit. I send them outside to play.

I deserve a reward. I resist.

While they're outside and I'm wrestling laundry out of the washer and into the dryer, the baby silently climbs the stairs and starts sticking his hand in the toilet, because this is one of the funnest entertainment ploys of all time—especially when it hasn't been flushed, which is the terribly frequent state of most toilets in my house. I discover him, along with the mess he's made, while I'm carrying clean clothes up the stairs, so I set to work cleaning. The twins peer in from outside and see that I'm not in the kitchen or anywhere they can see, because, to reiterate, I'm upstairs trying to wash the poop water off their baby brother's hands. The two of them decide this would make the perfect opportunity to steal inside the house, rummage through the cabinets, and pour all the homemade cleaners into a gigantic hole they and their brothers have been digging in the backyard. That's not enough, though. While I am still preoccupied with their brother and his disaster, they break into Husband's shed and find a gasoline can.

A quick aside: This has happened before. There were consequences. They don't care about the consequences. They break inside anyway.

Out comes the gasoline can, which they also pour into the gigantic hole. Husband was planning to use that gasoline to mow our lawn later today, because we got a note from our homeowner's association saying it was a little out of hand. Also, there's a shrub that needs trimming, the letter said. It didn't say which one of the eight in our yard they believe needs trimming, so we're just guessing. Unfortunately, it's not the one the twins, after dumping all the cleaners and gasoline into this hole, decided to cut with the shears.

They are herded inside and told to sit on the bench at the kitchen table. They smell like pickled gas pumps.

I need a reward. I barely resist.

Monday lunch

The only time my sons are still and quiet is when they have food in front of their faces—and barely then.

After lunch, I wrestle them into bed, for a few hours of blissful nap time when I pretend I can't hear the twins jumping off their bed and having a good old time before they crash in various chalk crime-scene positions on their floor or bed or wherever it is they collapse in utter exhaustion.

I don't need a reward. I can do this.

Monday afternoon

Fighting, shrieking, complaining about homework, someone says he hates me, someone else says he wishes he had different parents, especially a different mom, like I can't hear him, someone forgets to flush the toilet after a very loud unloading session on said toilet, making the whole downstairs smell like a sewage plant, someone else eats five apples without permission (which means he'll probably need the toilet soon).

Why are kids so hard?

I need a reward. I…resist.

Monday dinner

They're all complaining about dinner, and I am, too.

Why can't we have pizza? they say.

I don't know. I really don't know anymore. Why are we doing this to ourselves? Why are we torturing ourselves and our children trying to eat the food that is good for us but takes twice as long to cook and four times as long to complain about and tastes like…

Oh. It tastes pretty delightful.

(So would cookies.)

I deserve a reward for cooking this amazing dinner.

No! I've made it all day!

Must…press…on.

Monday bedtime

After stories and brushing teeth (during which time someone lands a glob of spit and mint toothpaste in the middle of the mirror I just cleaned), we wrestle them into bed. Three times.

We have to visit the twins' room four times, and the last time we enter, they've changed their clothes.

"Why did you change clothes?" I say.

"Because we accidentally peed," one says.

I look around. The floor is clean.

"Where did you put your clothes?" I say.

"Under there," the other says. He points under his baby brother's crib, where, when I bend down to look under it, I see a whole wad of clothes. I gag. It smells like a horse pasture under here. I don't think I even want to know.

I leave.

"Get back in bed," I say to the older boys as I pass through.

And just when we think they've finally settled down and are actually going to sleep, one of them bursts into the room and tells us he accidentally brought all his drawing supplies up to the library and one of his brothers stepped on a drawing pencil and broke it and now he's really, really sad.

I deserve the biggest reward.

I want to resist, but…

Monday before sleep

I'll start the thirty days tomorrow.

It's all good. I got this.

This is going to be easy.

The Entertaining Excuses Kids Make to Avoid Certain Foods

I am a lucky parent.

My kids have never historically been picky eaters. Ever since they were really little, they've been great eaters. Excessive eaters, maybe, but great. And this is saying a whole lot, because we don't eat the kinds of things I ate as a kid—which is to say, packaged foods. The first time my eight-year-old, who was four at the time, stayed the night with my mom and stepdad, he lectured them on how the cereal they were feeding him was made in a factory.

Yeah. We're THAT family.

We've relaxed a tad bit over the years, but I'm still obsessive about my kids' nutrition (along with their sleep and reading habits), and we haven't journeyed far from those early days: mostly vegetables, some meat, and no processed foods, except on cheat nights once a week.

Sometimes this makes my kids feel a little excluded, when their friends bring Goldfish and packs of chips for their afternoon snack at school and they get some cut celery with hummus. But, for the most part, they take it in stride. Husband says it's because hungry boys eat pretty much anything—which is a valid theory. I think, however, it's because of my endless lectures about health and nutrition, which have begun to sink in, but, you know, whatever.

All that aside, there are some things that our kids have, lately, refused to eat.

For instance, the other day we had some tasty roasted asparagus. Traditionally, our boys love asparagus. It has never gotten any complaints. It's just that they're not very good at eating it—chewing it, specifically. If you've ever shared a table with famished boys, you know that they *inhale* food, rather than chew it. And if you've ever had asparagus you might have noticed that it's a somewhat stringy vegetable. It needs to be chewed. For the inexperienced chewers, which describes all six of my sons, it's difficult to chew asparagus effectively without gagging or choking.

The other night, while we were all gathered around the dinner table, my oldest son shoved an entire sprig of asparagus in his mouth, in spite of a warning from yours truly, and he chewed it so inefficiently that, of course, he choked. It was a spectacular choke, too. When he tried to pull it back out of his mouth, it did not stop coming. It was like a magician's trick—the one where the magician pulls a whole tied-together string of scarves out of his throat. That asparagus did not have an end. It was the never-ending story of an asparagus.

We all watched with wide eyes. It was astonishing.

I gagged.

Now the oldest doesn't ever want to eat asparagus. I think

he might be worried he'll choke again. I keep telling him that if he just chews well, he won't have to worry about it, but he either doesn't believe me or he doesn't know what the word "chew" means.

The other day, my seven-year-old looked down at his salad and said, "This is, like, toxic to me. I can't breathe." He had just taken a bite, and I wanted to tell him that he probably couldn't breathe because he was trying, once more, to inhale his food, and some things, especially the fresh things, have to be chewed to be enjoyed.

I laughed at his melodrama, which he gets from his father, but he gave me a Look that said he was completely and utterly serious. He could not breathe, that salad was so toxic.

"Salad is good for you," I said. "It has lots of vitamins and minerals that help you grow big and strong." I have this line down.

"Not to me," he said, and he pushed his plate away.

One of the four-year-olds, to show he wanted to be big and strong, offered to eat what was left on his brother's plate. He shoved it all in his mouth and promptly gagged.

Guess it was toxic to him, too.

I get it. I can be a picky eater, when it matters. I don't like peas or corn or cabbage. Brussels sprouts make me vomit. I can't abide the texture of cantaloupe.

We all have our likes and dislikes. But if you're going to run a house full of children, it's impossible to cater to everyone's likes and dislikes. It's important for our kids to understand this.

They've gotten quite creative in the ways they refuse the foods they don't want to eat. Sometimes they say they're full, even though they've hardly touched anything on their plate and we know they're not anywhere close to full, especially when they follow up this declaration with, "May I please have a banana?" I will smile at them sweetly and remind them that if they are full, they have no more room for a banana. They look at me blankly.

Sometimes they'll come up with the line, "My throat hurts." At this point, I lecture them about The Boy Who Cried Wolf, because the next time their throat hurts, will we believe them?

"Yes," they say.

The lesson never quite sinks in.

Sometimes they deviate from the throat hurting and creatively substitute the stomach or the head. Sometimes they say they're too tired to eat.

I wish I could be too tired to eat. I'm tired a lot of the time, but I have never, ever been too tired to eat.

The best excuses are the ones where my kids claim they're allergic to something. The other day Husband added some cherry tomatoes to our avocado salad, and the seven-year-old said, "I'm allergic to tomatoes."

"Oh, really?" I said. "Since when?"

He shrugged and said, "I can't feel my face when I eat them. Or my tongue." He looked down at his finger. "Or my fingers when I touch them."

I shook my head on the outside, but on the inside, I was

congratulating him for his creativity. What a story.

I don't let any of this bother me. A wise pediatrician once told a young mother, who worried about her son who wasn't eating his carrots, that when a boy is hungry, he'll eat.

I believed him.

Eventually, my uncharacteristically picky eaters will cave.

Tonight we're having roasted beets. I wonder what sorts of excuses they'll find not to eat that.

On Leap Years: An Impossible Wish

This year happens to be a leap year.

For those of us who have been around for a while, this isn't that big a deal. We watch leap years come around every four years, and we watch them pass with an extra day, and nothing seems all that different.

My kids are out of their minds about this leap year thing, though. A day that only comes around once a year? they say in shocked disbelief.

Yeah.

What would you do if you had a birthday today?

Uncle Jarrod almost did.

He would only be a kid still?

No, the years still pass. Just because his birthday only rolled around every four years doesn't mean he'd stay frozen in time and quit growing.

They seemed relieved to hear that, even though they still didn't quite get it. In their minds, a person with a birthday on February 29 would stay forever young. So I showed them a picture of Dee Brown (the novelist, not the basketball player), who definitely grew older and died at the ripe old age of ninety-four and only technically celebrated one-fourth of those birthdays.

All I know is that if being born on Leap Day really meant you only aged a year for every four, I'd volunteer for that.

Well, maybe not. I'd only be eight. I was pretty annoying at eight, and that was also the year I got the most embarrassing purple glasses you've ever seen that took up half my face because it was the late eighties and people (I'm not naming any names, Mom) didn't feel the need to help their eight-year-old kid who needs glasses still look cool. The era took care of cool —as in crumpled it up and crushed it beneath a stiletto heel.

Anyway. That is not the point of this essay. The point of this essay is to consider leaping past a whole day in your life. You know, with years that are not leap years, February has the privilege of leaping over its last day like it doesn't even count.

Where do I apply to leap over a whole stretch of time? Because I'd like to sign up for leaping over Year Three With Twins.

Kids typically begin to develop minds and wills of their own around age two. Mine were easy to manage until age three. And most of my aged three children were not terribly difficult to manage.

Then came twins.

You know how three-year-olds ask a billion questions a day? Try having two of them. I'm so questioned out I could live the next thirty years without hearing another one, which is completely impossible in my current reality. I'll hear another billion questions by the time you finish this sentence.

Also, the number of times I've turned into a three-year-old

myself is quite astonishing. You'd think that after all these years, after having survived three other three-year-olds, I would know better than to engage in an argument with a strong-willed toddler. But I'm still a sucker for taking a threenager up on his challenge, mostly because they think they know everything, and *I'm the one who knows everything.*

I can get myself into a lot of trouble if I say something like, "Here's your vitamin."

"You mean my melatonin," one of the three-year-olds will say.

I don't like misinformation, because I spent a decade as a reporter, so, predictably, I'm quick to correct him.

"No, this is not melatonin," I say. "It's called Focus Factor. It helps you focus."

"No. It's melatonin."

"No. It's Focus Factor."

"It's melatonin!"

"I can read. You can't."

He'll argue for another twenty minutes. I need to learn to let things go.

"Mama, you're doing your workout wrong," one will say when I'm actually busting my rear end to get ahead of the workout video because I'm a beast.

No, I'm sorry, I know exactly what I'm doing and you should just shut your mouth if you don't want an uppercut right to your jaw. (Not because I'd beat a kid who tells me I'm slacking while my heart rate is camped at one hundred thirty. It's because I'm doing uppercuts during my workout, and he's leaning in way too close to tell me I'm doing it wrong.)

"I didn't have milk today" is another one of my twins' favorite things to say, even though the cup they're staring at right this very minute still has three drops of milk in it because they *just finished their glass.*

Um, yes you did.

"I'll put my jacket on," one of them said on a morning we were already five minutes late for leaving, and, hey, who am I to argue, because the sooner they figure out how to put on their own clothes, the sooner I don't have to do it. Except one of them likes to turn his jacket inside out before putting it on, which I'm pretty sure defeats the purpose. The wool doesn't make you warm when it's on the outside, dear.

"Your jacket's not on correctly," I said.

"Yes it is," he said.

"No it's not.

"YES IT IS."

"Okay, then wear it like that. Just don't complain about being cold."

Natural consequences for not listening to your mother who knows everything.

They talk back about everything, they have their own ideas about the way things should be (I want the BLUE plate. There is no blue plate. I want the BLUE plate. You can have the yellow plate or the orange plate. I want the BLUE plate! Okay, you get nothing), they make ridiculous threats (I not eating ever again, because you said it's still time to stay in our beds and I don't want to take a nap. Okay, more for me, then.), they fight about everything (This is Lightning McQueen. No, THIS is Lightning McQueen. It's the same car, guys.), they know everything, they break everything, they mess with everything, they can do everything themselves even if it means going the whole day with their shoes on the wrong feet.

So if I had to choose a stretch of time in my parenting that I could leap over, it would be Year Three With Twins. Potty Training With Twins comes at a distant second.

We're looking forward to Year Four With Twins, with high hopes that three will be long gone and we will have our sweet little twins back.

What's life without a little idealistic dreaming?

The Thing About a Strong-Willed Child

I have several strong-willed children. This isn't so hard to believe, considering I'm probably one of the most stubborn people you've ever met. At least that's what Husband says all the time when I'm trying to win an argument. There is no such thing as winning an argument with me; there is only getting shut down by my amazing argumentative abilities.

Not really. It's inaccurate to say there's no such thing as winning an argument with me. Husband wins about one percent of the arguments.

My oldest son inherited my strong-willed nature at a slightly higher concentration.

Have you ever engaged an argument with a strong-willed child? It's like attempting to convince a tornado it doesn't really need to traverse this particular path but could it please veer off in that other direction where there are no houses that could be destroyed?

Here's what the argument in our house looked like today (because they happen every day—sometimes multiple times a day):

Him: Can my friend come over today?

Me: Not today, buddy.

Him: Why not?

Me: I'm trying to fix dinner right now, and then after that, we'll be doing all our after-dinner chores and it will be time to start all the nighttime stuff, so…

Him: Just for a little bit.

Me: Not today. There's not any time. We'll find another time when he can come over.

Him: He could come over right after dinner. There will be some time.

Me: Like five minutes.

Him: That's enough.

Me: That's how long it would take him to walk over here. So no. Again.

Him: We would just be doing this one thing.

Me: I already said no.

Him: Please?

Me: Again, no.

Him: But if I promise to get in the bath as soon as he's gone?

Me: No.

Him: But we have to do this thing before school tomorrow.

Me: Nothing you say is going to make me change my mind. I know that you think it will, but has it ever?

Him: One time it did.

Me: Probably because you wore me so far down that my brain was a big fat mush and I couldn't think of anything else to say. But no.

[Half an hour later.]

Him: I finished my chore. Can my friend come over now?

Me: NO!

Him: This is the worst house ever. I wish I was in a different family.

He left in a huff, but that was not the end. It's never the end. He came back after a few minutes of strategic thinking and asked the same question in a different way.

If you are privileged enough to have a strong-willed kid, you know that they never, ever, ever let go of anything. Ever. They will press their point until it's nearly a wound in your side (and sometimes it is). And you will have to keep answering no to the same question asked a billion different ways, because they will keep at it and keep at it and keep at it.

When my son was really young, he would remember everything. If we told him it was time to pick up his coloring things and that he would be able to color with them when he woke up from his nap, the first thing he would say upon waking from his nap was, "Will you get out my coloring things for me?" He keeps a mental file of all the things that we have promised, and he visits them regularly. This has made us very careful about the things we promise our children—which is a good thing; I had a lot of promises broken as a kid, and it didn't set me up for a healthy emotional life as an adult—or even what we mention might be possible.

We get a lot of mileage out of our strong-willed child, and by mileage, I mean energy expenditure. Nothing has the ability to suck my energy dry in any given day than one or two or two-thousand arguments with my strong-willed child.

We don't say no to everything he asks, of course, because what kind of parents would we be if we did? That's not a fun house to live in, where you know your battle is over before it's started. The problem is that many of his requests and battles are for things that are simply not possible in our current reality.

Getting a dog.

Staying home alone.

Going over to a friend's house whose parents we haven't met.

He doesn't understand fully the reasons behind our no all the time, and many days it takes an hour of explanation to help him see the reasons we do what we do.

This can get exhausting.

Strong-willed kids will wrap around your last nerve and then take out the sharpest scissors they can find and snap it.

One day my son came home from school and was insisting that he didn't have any homework, but every time I went over his agenda, I couldn't help but notice that his teacher had written a homework assignment in red letters, on the day's space. The rule in our house is that you do your homework first and then you get to have a bit of technology time, after which time you are banished to the outdoors for the rest of the day (it's only an hour. They'll be okay.).

He wouldn't set down his insistence long enough to listen to what I was saying or read what his teacher had written. We argued for almost an hour before he finally said he'd already done the homework to which I was referring.

He didn't even see the irony in how much time we could have saved if he had just listened to what I was saying in the first place.

The other day he had to stay home from school because he had a stomach virus that lasted for about fifteen minutes before he was ready to start on his daily strong-willed exercises. I hardly got any work done, because he kept asking if he could have his tech time already since he was home from school.

No. Kids who stay home from school don't get tech time until the normal time.

But it would save time when his brothers got home.

No.

Please?

No, no, no, no, no.

Sometimes I wish I had my voice recorded in such a way that would interject a "no" into every one of his revised questions.

Strong-willed children are challenging children.

This is, after all, the kid who, at three, had a logical argument for why he shouldn't have to take a bath. I know where arguing with him gets us. It gets us running around in circles, trying to defend our rules and expectations and, in the process, requires us to take another look at why we actually have the rules and expectations we have. This is good for us. We, as parents of strong-willed children, get to constantly reevaluate our techniques and our philosophies and how we've chosen to raise our children, and we get to see whether or not our principles are still working for us and our family.

These qualities that annoy us so much on a daily basis will be assets to our children, when they are older. Strong-willed children are tender-hearted and persistent and focused and able to see every single loophole that exists everywhere. They're good at becoming the exception.

And these will all be advantageous traits when they're older. They're just difficult when our kids are three or five or ten and are not yet able to fully embrace the word "no" or before they gain the strategic ability to pick their battles.

One day they will. At least there's hope in that.

But I swear, if he asks me the same question a different way again, I'm going to regret I ever said I'm thankful for his persistence.

The Puberty Talk with Boys: an Official Transcript

Dad: Son, do you have a minute?

Son: I'm working on some LEGO buildings. But I guess.

Dad: We wanted to talk to you about something important.

Son:

Mom: We need you to listen really well.

Son: [break, snap, break, snap]

Parents: [to each other] You think he's listening?

Dad: It's probably better for him to be playing with something. This could get awkward.

Son:

Dad: Son, soon you'll be going through some changes. These are big, awkward changes, changes you probably won't want to talk about, so we wanted to tell you about them before you're actually going through them. It'll be easier on all of us, I think.

Son:

Parents: Are you listening?

Son: Yes. [break, snap, break, snap]

Dad: First of all, your armpits will start to smell. Oh, who are we kidding? Your armpits already smell. That's why we've been telling you to wear deodorant for a year. Are you wearing your deodorant?

Son: What's deodorant again?

Parents: [shaking heads]

Mom: Okay, we'll get to that. Body odor is bad. Use deodorant.

Son: Okay. You'll have to show me where it is.

Mom: I've shown you so many…never mind.

Dad: Your feet will grow and your legs will lengthen out. Sometimes this will happen disproportionately. You're a beanpole now, but you'll be even more of a beanpole later. Don't worry about that. You'll fill in the space. Time does a lot of things. I used to be like you, and look at me now.

Son: [poking Dad's stomach] Hahaha

Dad: [swatting son's hand away] Anyway.

Son: Hahaha

Dad: You can stop laughing now. This is serious.

Son: [returning to LEGO creations]

Dad: For a while you've been trying to gain a little muscle. I see you doing pushups around the house and trying to lift your brothers. Let me just tell you, muscles come in time, too. That's all a part of growing up.

Son: [whistling]

Dad: Are you still listening?

Son: [nods while continuing the whistling]

Dad: You'll probably start to feel a little awkward during

this time period, and parts of your body will grow, including your penis.

Son:

Dad: [clearing throat] You'll start to feel like maybe you like girls a little, but you should definitely stay away from them for a while, because your mother says there's no dating in this house until you're thirty.

Mom: Or maybe twenty-five. Okay, I guess we can make it twenty.

Son:

Dad: You'll start to grow hair in a lot of different places—maybe your chest, and your underarms, and, you know. [gestures to "down below"] You'll get some on your legs, and maybe on your chin, and you'll have to start shaving your chin and lip to make sure it doesn't get out of hand.

Son:

Mom: Hopefully, you'll start caring more about hygiene, but I'll just tell you, it's healthiest to take a bath about every other day. I think you average one or two a week, but that's bordering on the gross side of hygiene. You're starting to make our house smell, and I'm not exaggerating.

Son:

Dad: Some of these changes will be a little scary, but they're all perfectly normal. I went through them when I was around your age, and every man from now until the end of time will go through them, too. So just sit back and relax and enjoy the ride of puberty.

Son:

Dad: Did you hear anything we said, son?

Son: [looks at dad] My penis is going to grow? Like, really big?

Dad: Is that all you heard?

Son:

Dad:

Son: [shrug] Maybe.

On Chores: a Tale of Exaggeration and Evasion

Every evening, at around 6:15, you will hear my house erupt into a chorus of weeping, gnashing of teeth, and flop-sliding across a (very) dirty kitchen floor.

This is the time in our schedule known, affectionately, as Complain About After-Dinner Chores Time.

It doesn't matter how many times we've done this routine —we even have a reminder sheet posted in a convenient location in our kitchen that states, very clearly, "As soon as dinner is over, put your plate away and immediately begin on your after-dinner chores. Mama and Daddy will gladly accept payment for your chores if you choose not to do them." Still, my kids will act surprised when they're stretched out in the living room, reading a book, and Husband or I gently touch their shoulder and say, calmly (on the good nights), "Have you already done your chore?"

"What?" they'll say, like we haven't done this dance every single night since they first started doing chores when they were three.

"You have a chore, remember?"

The response to this is always, "I haven't had a night off in a long time."

Yeah, well, join the club, kid.

Lately, they've gotten very creative about trying to get out of these chores. As I'm bending over the sink trying to finish up the washing of twenty cups that six kids managed to dirty during the course of the day, they'll toss out their far-fetched excuses, and, to be honest, I don't have much empathy for them at the end of a day when I've taken knees and elbows into my side and back because I decided I was going to meditate on the floor during their reading time, which you should never, ever do in a house of boys.

Here are some of the excuses my boys have given their daddy and me for getting out of their after-dinner chore time.

1. "I hurt my leg."

To be more accurate, you could trade out "leg" with any other appendage or organ on the human body. It could be head, arm, stomach, booty, even penis sometimes. My boys have a wonderful grasp on anatomy vocabulary, which they showcase practically every night to get out of their after-dinner chores.

These hurts, however major or minor they may be, all make doing their chores impossible.

I wake up aching every morning now (getting old stinks), but I'm still expected to lean over the dishwasher and put the silverware where it goes when it's my turn on the schedule. Otherwise, no one would have any utensils to eat with. I know my boys wouldn't care about omissions like that, but I do.

The other day, as we were walking home from school, my oldest son was looking down at his leg, which he said was hurting a little, and, while he was looking down, he walked right into the limb of a tree. I tried not to laugh (it was very difficult) and then checked him over for damage. He was okay. The branch had narrowly missed his eye.

Guess what he used as his excuse that night.

This boy has a slight penchant for the dramatic, so that night he said, "You know I almost blinded myself today!" He pointed at the tiny little scratch beside his eye and said, "What if it gets infected and I lose my eye?"

Still doesn't excuse you from your chore tonight, buddy. One day at a time.

2. "I forgot I have homework."

This one is always fun, because (1) I hate homework and don't always feel like enforcing the completion of it, because I'd rather my sons be playing, and, also, they're in elementary school. It's unnecessary. And (2) they actually have ample time to do that homework in the afternoon. They're supposed to do their homework before they do anything else—before they have their designated technology time, before they go play outside with their friends, before they take out the LEGO collections and start building immaculate cities.

So if they tell us that they still have homework, our standard response is, "Well, I guess you'll have to get up early tomorrow and do it. Homework time has passed for today. Now it's time for after-dinner chores."

It might sound cruel (and they certainly think it is), but to reiterate, I don't really care about homework, and part of growing up is taking responsibility for the things you have to do. I can't micromanage them all their lives just to make sure they're doing their homework and turning it in. I don't have the energy or the patience.

3. "None of my friends have to do chores."

This phrase is usually coupled with the followup phrase, "This is the worst family ever."

If I were to listen to my boys on this issue, none of their friends would have to wear jackets in the winter, fold and put away their own clothes after they've done laundry, do their homework, take a bath, or pick up after themselves.

They especially don't have to wipe counters, wipe off the table, sweep the floor, load the dishwasher, put the dishes away, or take out the trash.

My standard response to this is a twist on the good old classic, "If your friend jumped off a cliff."

"It's a good thing you're not like your friends, then," I say. "Because if your friend jumps off a cliff, you'll have the foresight not to follow."

They never appreciate the irony of this statement quite as much as I do.

4. "I feel sick."

Usually this declaration comes on the heels of eating twelve pieces of pizza or five helpings of mashed potatoes. I think it's half falsehood, half truth. I'm sure their stomachs really *are* hurting, because they inhale their food so fast their stomachs don't have half a chance to tell them it's already full.

I'm not the least bit surprised they feel sick, but, unfortunately, that doesn't mean they're going to get out of their chores. I could barely stand up one day because the flu virus was ravaging my body, and I still had to wash the dishes because it was my turn. I felt like complaining all night, too, but I wanted to be an example. So I held up my head with one hand and used the other hand to load the dishwasher, because Toalsons are tough.

5. "My teacher said I had to ____."

Sometimes my boys will bring their teachers into things. My teacher said I had to do more homework. My teacher said I had to collect some dirt, and it will be too dark out there when we get done with the chores. My teacher said I need to bring a different kind of lunch tomorrow, which I'm going to pack right now.

Oh, what kind of lunch?

A lunch with cupcakes in it.

Huh. I didn't get that message.

Whatever it is they tell me their teacher told them to do, I usually follow up their declaration with the same answer I use for excuse number three.

6. "It's raining."

I'm not really sure what the weather has to do with doing chores (or, really, anything at all in our current place on the nighttime schedule). Maybe it's just an observation. But then the one on trash duty will look at me and say, "Well, I won't be able to take out the trash because it's raining."

A little rain never hurt anybody.

Sometimes one of them will say it's too dark to take out the trash; they'll have to do it tomorrow.

So I clear my throat and tell a true story: I had to carry laundry from my bathroom to a detached building and back again every time I was on laundry duty as a kid, rain or shine, day or night. I worked hard to get it all done before the dark descended upon the corn fields all around us, because you never knew what kind of horrors were living in those plants. They whispered things you didn't want to hear. (Yeah, I was an interesting kid.)

Weather is no excuse. Carry on.

7. "I'm tired."

I cannot truly capture the magnitude of my mirth when it comes to this excuse. Tired? They don't even know the definition of tired. Tired is wrestling six kids into bed when you can barely hold up your head because of the flu. Tired is getting up and cooking breakfast for your kids after you spent a night courting a particularly vicious stomach virus. Tired is trying to figure out how to do your day job after a toddler kept you up all night with his night scares.

That's tired.

Now. I know they have long days at school, and that can be tiring, sure. I empathize with this; if I had to spend all day around whole groups of people, I likely would have to peel myself up off the floor to fling myself into bed (which is usually what I do when it's my bedtime, and I only have seven other people in this house). I get that school is mentally and physically challenging and that walking a whole half mile to and from that school can also be tough.

But too tired to do a chore that will take ten minutes if you just suck it up and do it? Nope.

I don't know that we'll ever hear the end of excuses when it comes to chores. They'll probably just get a bit more sophisticated as my sons get older. But neither Husband nor I will ever give up this battle, because it's important that our children learn they're part of a family and that we need their contribution. It's important for them to know that what they do within the dynamic of our family's life is necessary, vital, and appreciated. It's important for them to know that they belong, here, with all of us. We are a team. We support our members. We do what needs to be done.

This is family life.

So until one of them comes home with a hatchet sticking out of his head (which happened to my cousin when we were kids; he was a boy), we'll be continuing to embrace our Complain About After-Dinner Chores Time every single night.

Mostly. Maybe I'll start wearing some headphones.

The Myriad Ways 'Seize the Day' Can Go Wrong

A wise man once declared to the world that we should all seize the day. Do it, he said, and you'll find success raining down on you.

I used to believe that mantra and the success it promised—until I had kids.

There are a thousand ways a day can go wrong with kids.

The baby could decide to snuggle and produce a masterpiece of a blowout, and, as you're walking him up the stairs, you realize the diaper is no longer fastened together but is, instead, dropping a trail of…well, you know what—all the delightful way to his room.

The four-year-olds could dig out a permanent marker from their brother's room and smuggle it into their room while you're preoccupied with cleaning up the disgusting you-know-what trail, and, while they're "sleeping" and you're putting up your feet for a few minutes of well deserved rest, they'll be quietly marking mustaches on each other's faces, which will make you the laughingstock of your sons' elementary school when you go pick up your older boys.

The older ones could be sneaking a snack every other minute so you won't have anything left over for their lunches tomorrow.

They could complain about dinner before they've even sat down to try it.

Or one of them could wake up with nothing more on his mind but to whine the entire day. It's like the song that never ends.

Take my today, for example.

Today, I climbed out of bed with high hopes for my week. We just spent a fun weekend with my mother, celebrating her birthday and visiting with my aunt and sister and brother-in-law and stepdad. There's nothing like a visit with family to launch you into the coming week, even if you did eat too many cupcakes at your mom's party. Today is Monday. Today is a Seize the Day kind of day.

These were my thoughts upon waking.

It wasn't a Seize the Day kind of day. Because after my workout, which was really hard, I was looking forward to at least half an hour of fixing breakfast all by my lonesome, a time during which I typically think or listen to an audiobook or stare into space without anyone needing anything from me. And then the nine-year-old got up half an hour early and came down to talk. All the words. I was worded out by 6:15 a.m. I finally told him that I'd like to listen to an audiobook and that he could talk to me in another fifteen minutes, when it was his scheduled time to wake up.

And then, of course, I felt guilty.

Add to this the fact that when I came down to make breakfast, there was hardly any preparation space because of the gigantic mess of papers and random stuff all over the counters. I realized then that there actually *is* a drawback to seeing family on the weekend: there's no motivation to unpack upon return.

So I found myself in the middle of a countertop mess, but there was also a mess on the dining room table and a mess spreading all over the space where I typically lay out my boys' school things so they can pack it all up themselves. I had to move all of that, which was not on the schedule for the morning, which put me incrementally later on my getting ready schedule.

Then I opened the fridge and realized that not only had we not reset for the week ahead, but we also hadn't gone grocery shopping. Mondays are supposed to be yogurt day, but there was only enough yogurt for one of the six, which is never, ever, ever a good idea in my house. Okay. Well, we had some leftover cereal, which they usually have as a "treat breakfast" on Saturdays. We could pretend like it was a "treat breakfast" kind of day. I poured them all a bowl of cereal and opened the fridge for the milk. There was less than a cup left. They had to eat dry cereal for breakfast.

I only hoped they wouldn't mention this to their teachers. They already dress like we're destitute.

Then the boys who hadn't yet risen did not want to get up, because it was raining so hard it was like they had a white noise amplifier outside their windows. I could understand that, because when my alarm clanged this morning, I also didn't want to get up. But we all had to do it. I dragged them out of bed, promptly after which the first grader complained about not wanting to go to school. I told him he had to. He said he had a belly ache. I said we'd talk after breakfast. He then went in search for his shoes, which are never where they're supposed to be, whining the whole way.

His shoes were outside. In the rain. Where he'd left them last night in his hurry to get a few minutes on the trampoline before it was time for baths.

I knew he wouldn't be able to retrieve them from outside, because it was pouring down so hard that when you opened the door, you already felt like you were getting pelted into the ground. Plus, mud.

So he had to wear flip flops.

Well, at least his stinky shoes got washed out in the rain. Even if he had to sit out during P.E.

After dropping off their brothers at school, my twins wanted to play outside, but it was still raining. So, instead, they played wildly inside, slamming doors, racing across couches, barreling over the baby. When I tried to lift my voice to be louder than the noise they were making, I strained a few vocal cords.

At nap time, I had to go into their room and scold them several times, because they were still so wired from not having any time outside in the Great Outdoors, which is essential to healthy living for boys and sane living for their mothers.

There were homework battles, they complained about

what was for dinner, no one could get a word in over the fighting volume at dinner (between kids, not parents), they filled the water to nearly overflowing at bath time and then used too much soap and, once out, didn't dry off all the way or wipe the floor where they'd stood, so when I walked into the bathroom to tell them, for the fourth time, that it was time to get out of the bath, I slipped and nearly did the splits. Which means tomorrow I won't be able to walk.

At bedtime, we had to remind them no less than six times that it was time to stop talking and go to sleep.

So, you see, a day can go really, really wrong. It can become such a train wreck, such a mangled mess, that you won't even recognize it by the time you get to the end of it. You'll wake up with all the positivity in the whole world, and then one of them will kick off a shoe, which another will trip over and bust his nose, which another will laugh about and be promptly hit in the face by the brother who actually likes the injured brother, and another will laugh so hard he chokes on a pita chip and you'll have to do the Heimlich maneuver to make sure he doesn't die, after which he'll likely yell at you for hurting his stomach and nearly breaking his ribs (hey, you're out of practice—which is a good thing, right?). It's a comedic twelve-ring circus every single day.

That's why the better way to win a day is to seize the moments.

The moment when he sits on my lap for story time, even though he's seven.

The moment when he lifts his hands to be picked up so he

can see the rain outside.

The moment when he says I look beautiful, even though I'm wearing the same old workout clothes I always wear.

The moment he is watching a cardinal outside the window and is enamored enough to leave his hand in mine for a minute.

The moment when they give all the women they encounter on their walk a purple wildflower, just to brighten their evening.

The moment when they say, "I love you," because the next moment their declaration could likely turn to "I hate you."

The moment when they're actually glad I'm their mom.

These are the moments parents can notice, seize, and keep. They are the moments that say, "I have lived this day to its fullest. And it was beautiful."

HILLS THAT ARE HARDLY HILLS

10 Things You Can Blame on Your Kids

All of us have our shortcomings. There is, perhaps, nothing truer than this. No one is perfect, after all.

For all the shortcomings I notice about myself (and there are a lot), probably about eighty percent of them are true, because I'm a child of divorce and suffer from self-esteem issues and blah blah blah, I don't want to bore you.

But this amazing thing happened when I became a parent: All of those shortcomings disappeared. That eighty percent dropped to zero percent.

How did I make that happen? Well, that's easy. I just blame everything on the kids.

Like

1. The smells.

Every now and again, I'll be in the store, perusing the aisles like any other shopper, except I'll suddenly inhale and realize my nose hairs are singed. "Oh my gosh," I'll say, loudly. "Did one of you toot?" The boys will look at me and collapse into giggles, because just the *idea* of a toot makes boys laugh, even if none of them claims it. They don't claim it because it was me. But the other shoppers don't know that. So I innocently continue on, cropdusting through the produce section, the healthy living section, the dairy section, and then on toward the checkout counter. Good thing I had my kids with me.

There are other smells I blame on my kids, but these are legitimate. Like how my house smells like a swamp because boys are really bad at aiming, and, apparently, flushing. Like how my backyard smells like a gas tank, because my four-year-olds managed to pick the lock on the shed out back and dump out the lawnmower's gas supply all over themselves and the grass so we could all go out in a blaze of glory. Like the sour milk/mildew/fart/dirty sock smell that wafts out into the world every time we open our van doors because, well, boys. It's like the air freshener you always wanted in your Honda Odyssey, one that tells the story of a family. I know I'll miss it when it's gone. I guess it's a good thing it never is.

2. The state of our house.

The reason our house looks like a paper supply manufacturer blew up in it is because my kids enjoy creating colorful forts out of construction paper when they're supposed to be in bed and Husband and I have already fallen asleep. It has nothing to do with the fact that I'm too lazy to get a trash bag out and sweep it all into the recycling. It also has nothing to do with the fact that I might have heard them out of their beds last night and I was too exhausted to investigate. All those papers? They make great sliders when I'm lifting weights, so win win.

My kids are also the reason everything in my house is broken. The coffee maker didn't explode because I poured water in the wrong slot. It exploded because my kid sneezed on it. The toilet didn't stop flushing because Husband had a massive sit-down for which he needed a whole roll of toilet paper. It stopped flushing because one of the four-year-old twins looked at it. That hole in the wall did not appear because I accidentally threw a shoe toward the shoe basket and missed by about five hundred yards. It appeared because boys weakened the drywall by touching it.

The door won't open all the way? The fan is missing a blade? The kitchen chair collapsed? Come on, kids.

3. The state of my yard.

Kids are the reason we hardly ever get around to mowing our yard. Do you know how hard it is to muster up the energy to pick up all the crap kids leave outside and know there's still something else you have to do? (I suspect you do know, if you're a parent.) So after you've spent three hours playing "Search and Find all the Hot Wheels" because your backyard turned into a wilderness, you're supposed to mow and weed eat and edge? No thanks. My ugly yard is the fault of my kids.

And not just the overgrown grass and the tree-weeds and the rose bushes that reach for you when you knock on our door. Also the holes you'll trip in when you're trying to play that Search and Find game in the backyard. My kids are using table spoons to dig a hole to the earth's core. I know, because they told me. Also, I fell in the hole, and Husband had to pull me out with a rope.

I think they're almost there.

4. Being late.

It doesn't matter how early we get up to go somewhere or how prepared we are for the day, shoes lined up just so, outfits picked out, breakfast already in the refrigerator, waiting to be warmed. We're going to get in the car at least fifteen minutes late—and that's a good day. All my sons could have every single bag in the world packed, and they would still remember something they need to "go back inside" to find. Someone will have to use the bathroom—number two. Someone else will spill their water all over themselves and scream until they get a change of clothes, because they don't want to "wear wet underwear all day!" Someone else will squeeze out a fart and accidentally shart.

Kids make parents late. Don't worry. You'll never remember how to get anywhere on time once you've been through the circus kids perform on the way out the door. So just sit back and relax and blame it on the kids.

5. Why I never get out of the house.

I'm not trying to make it seem like I have it harder than anyone else, but trying to get a family of eight out the door to go anywhere is like trying to give directions to monkeys and trusting they'll do what they're told. It's over before it began. Our friends are always inviting us to different activities around town—the park, the library, Six Flags—and it sounds so fun. We feel the longing. But thinking about the *work* of it is enough to make us say no. Our friends might not understand, but when you live in a house where, in five minutes, kids can change their clothes fourteen times, break into the chalk supply and leave their mark on every surface in the bathroom, and make three thousand paper airplanes out of the bills that came in the mail (that's okay, kids. We'll just pretend they didn't come), you don't really have the energy left to get out of the house.

I am a hermit because I have kids.

6. The rapid deterioration of my brain.

I used to be able to hold my own in the intelligence department. I don't say that to brag. I knew what the square root of sixty-four was. I knew what three times fifteen was. I knew what entropy was and how it was explained using physics (though I never truly understood its potency until I had kids). Now? My kids ask me how many pieces of pizza Suzy had if there was pizza with thirteen pieces and Margie had three of those pieces and Terrance had fifteen. I get all nervous, because I DON'T KNOW. I don't know how to solve their math anymore. I aced college algebra, but I can't do a second-grade math problem.

See, here's some math for you. I had a whole brain. I had six kids. Each of those six kids got a piece of the brain. How much of my brain is left?

The answer is: not much.

7. The stains on my shirt.

No, I'm not a messy eater. I just have kids who like to touch me with food on their hands.

You'll never actually know if this is true or not, because I've sworn Husband to secrecy. Only the two of us will know that the last time we went out on a date (which I can hardly remember, it was so long ago), I dropped jalapeño ranch dip all down the frontside of my shirt, and there was no kid within fifteen miles of that restaurant. Only the two of us will know that when we swung by the froyo place for a tasty treat, we ate it in the car, and when I turned on the light to check my face, there was a string of chocolate ice cream clinging to my shoulder (I'm pretty sure Husband flung it in his excitement to shovel a mouthful in his face). No one will know that when I'm huddled in my pantry, eating a handful of chocolate chips Husband hasn't found yet, I'll end up with the evidence on the top of my thighs. The shorts that cover my thighs, that is. I mean, on the thighs, too. A moment on the lips, forever on the hips. Who cares?

8. My physical state.

If I look like I'm too tired to be alive, it's because of the kids. If I look like I haven't brushed my hair in three weeks, it's because of the kids. If I look like I'm wearing the same clothes I was wearing yesterday and the day before that and maybe even the day before that, it's because of the kids.

I hang out all the time in workout clothes. I would wear something else, really, but in order to raise little boys, you have to be fast. And being fast doesn't happen in nine-inch heels and a cute little skirt. Being fast happens in neon pink Adidas shoes, running pants, a sports bra, and an oversized T-shirt. This is how I save my kids' lives. I'm ready to run any time they decide to do something completely stupid, which is pretty much every other minute.

Why do I have so many gray hairs? Kids. Why is my stomach a bit larger than it should be? Kids. Why do I look like I'm the walking dead? Kids.

9. Missing supplies.

I stopped signing my boys' school folders about three months before school was out for the summer. This is definitely not because I forgot. I remembered every morning. I just could never find a pen. And when I did happen to find a pen, it was only because the said pen did not have any ink left in it, and the boys could not be bothered to throw the pen away, so, inevitably, when I would be searching for something with which to sign their field trip permission slips, because that was a nonnegotiable when it comes to signing or not signing, I would stumble across the pen that was, unbeknownst to me, empty of ink and hear the victorious anthem of *Braveheart* in my head, right before bending over, putting the pen to paper, and realizing I had not, in fact, been saved.

So their permission slips got signed with blue crayon. I gave up on the rest of the folders.

10. Going to a Fresh Beat Band concert.

I only bought tickets because I have kids. It's not because I think the Fresh Beat Band is the coolest kids band ever and every time one of their songs comes on I want to break out dancing. (Well, so what if it is?)

If you see me playing with the build-a-house blocks at the San Antonio Children's Museum, it's because of the kids. If you see me dressing up like a royal queen in a too-short cape at the Witte Museum, it's because of the kids. If you see me playing with LEGO pieces and building a Star Wars Desert Outpost, it's because of the kids.

The truth of the matter is that we all make mistakes. We all have imperfections. Who am I to hold you in judgment? Who are you to hold me in judgment? We're all just doing the best we can, so we should embrace our mistakes.

Because as long as we have kids, we can blame EVERYTHING on them.

When You Feel Like Your Kids Don't Need You Anymore

It's good to feel needed as human beings. We need to feel needed, at least some of the time. It's how we recognize our value in our specific worlds.

Kids need parents for practically everything—at least for a while. They need us for crossing the street, even though they're nine and have done it a thousand times before (they probably just got lucky there were no cars coming all those other times). They need us to tie their shoes, or, if they're not feeling lazy today, to at least stand there and watch them do it on their own. They need us to watch when they're flipping over the side of the couch in what looks like a professionally-trained gymnast move, because if no one sees them, did they really just do it?

When kids start growing up and doing things for themselves, it can feel a little disorienting to suddenly have so much more time on your hands in the mornings. You no longer have to make their breakfast because they popped a slice of toast in the toaster oven and spread half the stick of butter on it when it was done. If you're anything like me, you'll feel a little sad that they're not whining about how you're not pouring their glass of milk fast enough because they just did it for themselves. You might even feel a little sad when they don't forget their lunch as they're walking out the door to school because they've finally learned the routine, after four years of practicing.

It sounds crazy to think that kids' independence would cause a parent sadness. Isn't independence what we crave when our three-year-old follows us around the house scream-crying for the toy his brother took away or our five-year-old bursts into the bathroom because he didn't "want us to be scared while we were going pee?"

Well, it happens. Trust me. Now that my nine-year-old takes a shower in the morning and I don't have to check behind his ears to make sure he actually used soap, I feel a little sad that I have three extra seconds on my hands.

But if you ever start feeling too sad about your kids' emerging independence, all you have to do is get on the phone. This will provide the perfect opportunity for them to engage in a heated argument about the red LEGO piece one of them took from another—because none of the other five billion red LEGO pieces in their collection will work—and, even though you've taught them effective methods of conflict resolution, they won't be able to resolve this argument with anything but a good old-fashioned fist fight. And the person who will most likely be on the other end of the line is a receptionist for your kids' pediatrician's office, who will politely try to ignore what's going on in the background even while you're asking her to please repeat the confirmation for that appointment, for the fourth time.

You could also press play on an audiobook or a podcast you've been meaning to listen to or (bless you) sit down to actually read a book while your boys are outside, entertaining themselves with sidewalk chalk. You can be sure that as soon as your finger hits the play button or your backside hits a chair, one of your children will come screaming into the house because he tried to smash the blue stick of chalk under a giant rock and he accidentally missed and smashed his toe instead and now it's probably going to fall off and he actually wishes it would, because he can feel his heartbeat in his pinkie toe.

Well. At least you read a whole sentence this time.

You could sit down on the toilet. That's when your kids will need you to get something down from a cabinet they can't reach—like a cup, which they'll use, as soon as you disappear back into the bathroom, to fill with water, submerge twelve LEGO pieces and the house keys (without mentioning this to you), and stick in the freezer just to "see what happens."

Or you could sit down to eat at the same time everybody else in your family sits down to eat. What a luxury, right? You no longer have to eat cold dinners. Unfortunately, this is probably the time when your kid, who's been drinking out of a regular cup for three years now, will accidentally knock over a brimming-with-milk Iron Man cup, because he was trying to reach across the table for more spaghetti before he's even inhaled his first helping. And you'll have to do what you've always done. Hand him the paper towels, watch him mop it up (not much more skillfully than when he was three), and then mop up behind his mopping, because perfection is the name of your game.

Or maybe just start talking to your partner, assuming that, because the kids are capable of caring for themselves now, they won't need you and you can actually finish a whole conversation in one sitting. But this is when they'll remember that they forgot to tell you an entire minute-by-minute narrative of how their day went, and even though they'll politely wait for you to finish before they'll start their story, they'll also stare at you the whole time they're waiting, and you can actually feel that wide-eyed gaze burning holes in your head, stealing your thoughts. You'll look at your partner, shrug, and listen to the random observations of a six-year-old before trying to remember what it was you needed to say to the other adult in the room (it will take you three days to remember).

Or you could try to go to sleep. And then they'll knock on your door with such urgency that you think this must surely be an emergency, and you'll fly out of bed, fling the door open, and see before you no one who is bleeding, passed out, or dying, or any kind of fire anywhere to be found—all emergencies as defined by your Family Playbook. No, sorry, baby, your stuffed animal losing a back leg because you and your brothers were playing tug-of-war with him is not an emergency. Go back to bed.

Get used to your kids doing anything on their own, and actually start missing the times when you were needed, and almost without fail, they will make sure you feel needed again.

Think I'm kidding? Start missing changing your baby's diaper. Someone in your house will wet their pants in no time.

It's no easy thing to pass from the I-need-you-all-the-time stage to the I-need-you-sometimes stage and then, inevitably, to the I-don't-need-you-at-all-anymore stage. It's also hard not to wish for an easier stage when you seem to be stuck in the I-need-you-all-the-time stage. I've been stranded there for almost ten years. I'd like to sit down for five minutes, please.

Also, stop growing up so fast, kids.

Just five minutes where you don't need me? Five seconds?

But here, let me do that for you, baby.

Lies We Believe as Parents: a Cautionary Investigation

Every now and then, I reach this mysterious place where parenting feels really easy. The boys are behaving perfectly (as if that's the measure of easy parenting), and everyone is loving each other well and, most importantly, no one is complaining about what I just put on the table for dinner before they've even tasted it. We are all a happy family. I like them. They like me.

It doesn't happen often, but when it does, I rejoice. And then they wake up completely different people the next day, and I find I've told myself a whole parcel of lies like this one:

I have really easy kids because I'm a really good parent.

Fortunately, this one gets debunked quite regularly by my oldest son, who is a practiced diplomat who never lets an answer stay an answer until he's rolled it all over the ground and wrestled it to near death.

After nine years of parenting this kid, I know better than to believe this lie. I don't have really easy kids because I'm a really good parent. I have really easy kids because they were born easy. I have a few of these in the mix, and they're delightful. They're also easily forgotten, because they don't require as much work. I could leave the six-year-old home all day alone, and the only thing I'd have to worry about is the state of the refrigerator when I got back (this kid once ate three pounds of red grapes when I raced upstairs to take a record-breaking two-minute shower). The others, well. They'll argue with a sock, if it told them to put it on.

There are a lot of other lies we tell ourselves, too. Like:

It's going to get easier.

This lie is your lifeline when you're the parent of twins. You spend the first year telling yourself it's going to get easier, because they'll be able to feed themselves, and then you spend the next year saying it'll get easier when they're three, because they'll understand things like "Don't take the baby-proof cover off that light socket. It will kill you," and then you spend the whole third year dying, because you have not known fear until you see three-year-old twins with their guilty faces on standing outside a bathroom door they just closed, saying they did "nuffing."

It's not ever going to get easier. I'm just going to tell myself that, and then maybe I'll be pleasantly surprised (but probably not).

The other day I found myself thinking of another lie while I was scrubbing the plate that had somebody's sour ranch dressing caked on it.

Eventually they'll do the chores to my standards.

Eventually they'll do the chores, that much is true. But it will probably not be up to my standards, ever. I know, because

I remember myself as a child. My mom had a rotating dish schedule, and after my shift, the sink was always splattered with water, and my mom told me over and over and over again that part of the dishwasher's job was to wipe up all the excess water, but yeah, yeah, I just wanted to get on to the part where I got to sit on the couch and read a book. Streaming audiobooks wasn't a possibility back then. If it had been, it would have been a different story, Mom.

Then, the other night, when I'd finished a dinner of sautéed chicken with mushroom and garlic sliced small enough so no one would complain about the unknown grossness caking their otherwise perfect meat, somebody, before he'd even tasted it, said he didn't like what we were having and he wasn't going to eat, and I discovered another big, fat lie.

One day they'll stop complaining.

I know this is a lie because the other day, when something was taking too long on my computer I started complaining about how you'd think we'd have faster computers in this century and this was ridiculous, it was taking *so much time* and I didn't have extra time at my disposal and I wish I could just hire someone to do this part and blah blah blah blah blah.

The only way my kids will stop complaining is if I magically somehow stop complaining, which is probably not going to happen anytime soon, because have you seen the mess kids can make in two seconds of inattention? Complaining about it is my livelihood.

On Christmas morning this year, I found myself agreeing

with the lie flipping through my head when my kids emptied their stockings and asked to eat a peanut butter cup.

It's only a little sugar.

"Only a little sugar" is like saying, "It's only a few broken pieces of furniture and a few more holes in the walls and a few whiny kids at the end of the day." Giving kids sugar is like rubbing yourself with raw meat and walking out into the African bush. You're going to die.

And, of course, we decided to have our first Family Fun Day on the first day of the new year, because the word we chose to frame this year is "play," and we wanted to end the boys' Christmas vacation on a good note: a day when we would all be able to enjoy each other and play.

Twenty minutes into that day I found another lie sneaking in, like maybe I wasn't paying attention:

One day it'll take us less than thirty minutes to pack up and get in the car.

It seems like the time it takes us to leave our house has progressively lengthened as my boys get older, because now they all have wills of their own. There is, of course, always another shoe to be found. There is always a drink someone forgot. But, as they increasingly get older, there is also always something they need to "pack up real quick" because they want to take a billion art supplies, three books, and five LEGO mini figures to the zoo.

Some lies knock us right off our parenting pedestals, like this one:

Not giving in to bad behavior makes bad behavior

magically disappear.

Oh, if parenting could be so simple.

I remember the first time this illusion was shattered for me: when my oldest threw a major fit because he wanted a green plate instead of a blue one. But the blue plate was the only one clean. And thus began the oft-repeated phrase in our home: "You get what you get, and you don't throw a fit."

I didn't give in then. Of course not. The tantrums would go away.

Except the tantrums did not go away. In fact, I suspect my oldest son tried harder. And I stuck to my boundary harder. And we danced for much longer the next time. And the next time and the time after that. Now he's nine. We don't fight about the green plate instead of the blue plate anymore. We fight about things like how he needs five more minutes of technology time to finish this one thing, even though his time's up.

Not giving in never solved anything in my house.

Every now and then, when a kid is talking about how they want to run away and how they wish they had different parents, I find myself thinking:

One day they'll understand.

One day they'll understand the boundaries we set; and one day they'll understand why we said no, their friend can't come over today because we want to spend some time together as a family; and one day they'll understand why we limit that technology time and require creative time before they earn it. But even if this is yet another parenting lie we believe, that doesn't change the fact that:

One day they will know just how much they were, are, and always will be loved.

I've gone over and over this one, examined it inside and out, and I've come to the conclusion that it cannot be a lie. They may not understand the love of everything we do right now, in this moment, but one day they will. I'm certain of it.

Now, excuse me while I go fish out of the toilet a stuffed animal that wanted to "take a mud bath" in the present someone forgot to flush. I'm sure it's going to get easier.

The Problem with Volunteering While Playing Parent

Every now and then I find it really hard to say no to volunteering.

That's a slight underestimation. I actually find it hard to say no at all. This is probably one of the biggest reasons why, when I walk my boys to school, I try to avoid all eye contact with their teachers and the parents who are volunteering to keep kindergarteners from becoming human tornadoes in the hallway: I don't want to be roped in and be challenged to exercise the power of no.

It's unfortunately not a power I possess.

It's a power I need to possess, a muscle I need to exercise, a stand I need to take on all things unnecessary.

But we learn by degrees.

One day, when someone texted Husband and me about leading worship at our sons' elementary school See You At the Pole, which is an event in Texas where kids, parents, teachers, and administrators meet at a flagpole and pray for their schools, I knew I couldn't say no. The ask was done over text, so it would have been easy, but we've done this event every year our boys have been in elementary school, and not doing it again would have felt, at best, weird and, at worst, terrible. So I said yes, we'd do it, knowing that we were in for it once we got there.

I'm usually the one strapped with all the boys during an event like this one, mostly because Husband has a much louder singing voice and also plays the guitar, while I only play the bass guitar. Past experience has angled me way in the back of the crowd, trying to concentrate on the program while my kids do what all kids do when their parents are otherwise occupied: climb up the flagpole stripped to their skivvies, because they're Captain Underpants.

What? Oh. Maybe that's just mine. And, for your information, it only takes a second.

Parents of young children should simply not volunteer to do anything—unless, of course, you have perfect children. I have one of those. When my twins go to school, I'll be able to volunteer for everything I want, because the baby is the most accommodating child I've ever had.

The problem with volunteering when you have typical children—which is to say those children who watch to see if you're looking and as soon as you aren't, they do exactly what you've told them not to do—is that when you're volunteering, your eyes are elsewhere. And they know this. And they use it— to their advantage, never yours.

You can see this in small snippets when you try to have a conversation with one of the moms in the after-school pickup line or when you pick up the phone and try to call your sister for a minute or when you optimistically (laughably so, in retrospect) think you can take some minutes to clean the house while your kids are occupied in the next room.

Here's a sampling of things my kids did with my divided attention the morning I volunteered for See You At the Pole:

1. Draw faces on cars in the parking lot.

Every time we're walking in a parking lot, at least two of my kids have this uncontrollable urge to touch other people's cars. No matter how many times we have told my twins not to put their hands on other people's vehicles—not only because it's not hygienic but also because it's someone else's car and not their own property—they have a very difficult time remembering this small piece of information. While my attention was divided, one of them marched up to a black sports car (we drive a silver minivan), drew smiley faces on the bumper, and then tried to get in the back seat. When I asked him, later, what he was doing, he said, "I was trying to get something out of the car." I'm not sure if he's lying or just really confused. You can never really tell with four-year-olds.

2. Explore the perimeters of the unknown.

I am hyper-vigilant when it comes to the possibility of my children getting lost. Before we go anywhere, I grill into my kids that they must never lose sight of me or, better yet, move out of my sight. Stay close, I say. Wait for your family, I say. Don't ever go somewhere that we are not, I say.

But I have two wanderers on my hands (the same two mentioned above). Once, they both disappeared at a local museum and we searched for nearly half an hour before they came running and grinning out of an elevator they were never supposed to get on. They were three.

The panic a mother experiences when one of her children disappears is nearly indescribable. Add to that panic an anxiety disorder, and you have a formula for a mom who's already imagined the worst—they were run over, they were taken, they were lost in the woods and are on their way to the highway—while they're blissfully on the other side of the school, shrieking on the swings.

Again: It only takes a second. I closed my eyes for a second—it may have even been half a second—and they were gone.

3. Say embarrassing things.

This usually happens at the close of any volunteering time: someone says something along the lines of, "Your boys are so wonderful. They're so well behaved and sweet," and then those wonderful, well behaved, sweet boys will use the space between this compliment and whatever gracious comment their mother would say in return to squeeze out the loudest fart in the history of farts (also the smelliest) and then laugh maniacally about this accomplishment. They'll then say something about how before they came here to this event, they sat down on the toilet and their poo was green with little orange flecks in it that they think were carrots. They'll say you yelled at them this morning on the way out the door, because you didn't want to be late and they didn't know how to put on their shoes (They do. They're just playing the sympathy card.).

So much for compliments.

Since my kids are likely not going to stop being

opportunists anytime soon, I think maybe I'm just going to have to give up on volunteerism for now. Practice that power of no. Maybe when they're older and we can all participate together, we'll try this again.

My kindergartener's teacher just asked me if I could help out with this year's holiday party.

I said yes.

If the Wishes and Dreams of Children Came True

We all make wishes and we all have dreams. It's the most hopeful part of the human condition, to wish and dream. But when those wishes and dreams land in the hands of children, well, we have a different animal entirely.

My kids make wishes and dreams all the time. But do they make sense? Are they noble? Would they change the state of the world? Meh. It's arguable.

If the dreams of my children came true, we would all weigh one thousand pounds.

This is because one of the recurring dreams of my children is to live in a world where breakfast is chocolate and lunch is chocolate and their afternoon snack is chocolate and dinner is chocolate and their nighttime nibble, if they had one, would be chocolate. In their world, every meal, every drink, every single thing on earth would be made of chocolate.

Now. I'm not saying I wouldn't like to live in this fantasy world, too, but I also happen to care about a little thing called health, and if all my kids eat is chocolate, the top floor of our house will no longer hold us. Also, have you seen my kids on sugar? If all we ever ate was chocolate, I'd need another fourteen hands. And another shot at sanity.

If the dreams of my children came true, they would own all the things.

It's somewhat horrifying how many things my kids want. You'd think we had taught them better than this, but, alas, it seems they have not yet learned the oft-repeated lesson of "be grateful for what you already have, because there are children going to bed hungry in other countries."

If one were to ask my children what they dream of most, you would hear things like "all the new Beanie Boos" or "all the Pokémon cards in the whole world" (If you haven't had the pleasure of being introduced to Pokémon, you are really missing out. There are more than a billion of these cards in existence, and if it were up to my nine-year-old, he would own them all) or "LEGOLAND right in our house." While it would be wildly impressive to live in a house completely made of LEGO bricks, I'm not quite sure that any kind of structure made of plastic—particularly if it's a home—would stand up to the abuse of six boys for more than a week. And that's being generous.

If the dreams of my children came true, the only music we would ever listen to is Kidz Bop or Minecraft music (Take popular songs! Add Minecraft lyrics! It's delightful!).

If we tried listening to our 1990s Pandora station, which the nine-year-old calls "the worst music ever. It's so bad it's killing my ears," all systems would shut down. And if all we listened to was Minecraft music all the time, I can guarantee I'd become one of those zombies—creepers, I think they're called —you're supposed to kill. Might as well shoot me now.

If the dreams of my children came true, they would never have homework.

Huh. You know what? That's one of my dreams, too.

If the dreams of my children came true, the three-year-olds would be allowed to do everything and anything for themselves.

This means it would take fifteen years to leave the house, because not only would we have to wait for them to button their jeans, but we'd also be waiting for them to figure out how to turn the sleeves of their jackets right side out. In this perfect world according to my children, they would be allowed to cross streets on their own and run through parking lots without holding a parent's hand and ride the elevator whenever they chose, because they wouldn't have the annoying rule about "staying within sight." They would be allowed to jump in the river after the bread they just threw at ducks, and they would be allowed to chase geese down a hill where a whole flock of them is waiting, and they would be allowed to climb over the rails at the zoo so they could go wading with the black bear.

They would, essentially, be able to accidentally kill themselves at will.

If the dreams of my children came true, they would be able to watch some kind of screen all hours of the day, every day.

They would be able to watch so many hours of Netflix and

Amazon Prime that their brains would cave in. They would be able to play video games until their brains started frying in the oil of inactivity and overstimulation ("This is your brain. This is your brain on screens."). They would be able to dive into their phones without talking to anyone around them for years.

On second thought, that sounds almost…nice. Hang on while I rethink this one.

If the dreams of my children came true, we would never have such things as naps and quiet time, and, God help us, bedtime.

Kids like to squeeze as much good out of a day as they can, which means they would gladly give up naps and quiet time and sleeping at all.

Me? I just want to get two seconds alone where I can think a coherent thought without someone interrupting me with a crisis like "My brother peed in the trash can."

And bedtime? If it were up to my kids, they would be able to stay up all hours of the night. They would not need sleep at all. They would walk around trying to remember where they last put down the baby, whining about how untidy the house is and how they're too exhausted to do anything about it.

Oh, wait. That's me.

I'm sure their dreams will become more refined over the years. Maybe they'll even get to hang right up there with Martin Luther King, Jr., inspiring people to dream for themselves and make change and dare to love.

Or maybe I'm just kidding myself and the only thing they'll ever want is the newest model Apple product.

So much for lofty dreams.

I Have a Dream, Too: a Digression

Today is a day we celebrate a great man of history who envisioned a lofty dream for America, one of peace and love and equality, spread to every corner of the world.

I appreciate and honor the legacy of Martin Luther King, Jr., but I have to admit that I'd forgotten today was a holiday until I woke up at four in the morning and couldn't get back to sleep, so I thought I'd check my email and then happened to read the note from my kids' principal reminding me that school was out for the day. Yay! My favorite. (In my defense: what parent can ever remember what day it actually is? If you can, congratulations. My brain doesn't hold unnecessary information like that.)

I lay in bed, trying desperately to get back to sleep, since there was at least an extra hour (surely kids would sleep in), while Husband clearly didn't have any trouble ignoring my insomnia, judging by the noises hurtling from his mouth and nose. So, naturally, I tossed and turned, thinking about King, which led me to think about my own dreams.

I ran through them—writing dreams, book dreams, music dreams, dreams for my kids, dreams for Husband—and when I'd listed them all in my much-too-busy-for-four-a.m. head, I thought about the one I've been wanting for quite a while now. It is simple at its heart: a good nights' sleep.

You might say I willingly gave up my right to a good nights' sleep as soon as I had six kids, because kids are kids, and then kids become teenagers and teenagers become adults and even when they're all sleeping through the night, finally, teenagers will go out on dates and hang out with friends, and adults will never call. I"ll never stop worrying about them until the day I die.

That's fair. But it's rare that anxiety or worry leads to a terrible nights' sleep, at least for now. Usually I'm so exhausted by my day and all the words that have bombarded me that I fall into a sleep that comes easily.

Our kids have always been champion sleepers, ever since they were tiny babies. It was highly out of the ordinary for a Toalson baby not to sleep all the way through the night by, at the latest, eight weeks of age. I know. I'm incredibly fortunate, and I recognize that.

It's also rare that any of my boys will wake in the middle of the night with nightmares or sickness, although it does happen on occasion. And when it does, well, I don't have any trouble rubbing a boy's back if he's not feeling well or posting up at their side until they feel safe enough to fall asleep or holding the baby if his gums are hurting him too much to sleep.

Those are not the reasons I don't always get a good nights' sleep.

I don't always get a good nights' sleep because of the simple fact that I sleep with a lawnmower.

I can't even count the number of times I have woken in the middle of the night and thought that one of my neighbors had mistakenly set their yard guy as their alarm clock and then, when reason climbed back to its rightful place and I turned toward Husband and felt the wind of his breathing flattening the top of my hair, the real culprit stepped forward. Metaphorically, that is.

There are nights when Husband will roll over and put his arm around me, and it's one of my favorite things to momentarily wake up and feel his warmth. But woe to me if I don't find sleep before he starts revving his motor, because I will have no hope of finding it for the remainder of the night. Sometimes he'll turn over on his stomach, which he says is better for the snoring thing, but I'd like to report that no, it's not. It muffles the sound just a tad, but it definitely does not eliminate it.

That is one magnificent yard he's mowing.

So, as we remember the contribution to history that Martin Luther King, Jr., made, I'd like to ask the powers that be to please, please, please solve this snoring problem, because I did not sign up for a John Deere tractor chime on my alarm.

Just before pushing Husband onto his belly this particular morning, I remembered that I'd recorded last night's one-man performance, because Husband didn't believe he could possibly be snoring as badly as he is. He seems to think I exaggerate a little.

I stuck a headphone in my ear and played the recording. I was surprised to find that there were two lawn mowers in our room last night. I have no idea who the other one was.

I was too afraid to investigate. Instead, I just rolled over and went back to sleep.

A Parent Never Really Knows What to Do: a Sticky Truth

You'd think that, at a certain point, when you've been a parent for a certain number of years or you're the parent of a certain number of kids, there would come a time when you actually knew what you were doing. But we had our sixth baby a little more than a year ago, and while some things are easier this time around, I can still say, with certain certainty, that even on the sixth kid, I have no idea what I'm doing.

See, the thing about parenting is that a whole lot of it comes down to the children. There's not one single thing that's going to work for every parent and every child, because there's no one archetype of "child" to point the way. I know. Our home is like a controlled experiment, a laboratory for testing out parenting practices. There's the strong-willed nine-year-old, who will challenge every single thing out of each parent's mouth, because he always sees things differently; there is the seven-year-old, who can't possibly stay out of candy if it's anywhere in the house, even if he's been told not to touch it; there is the six-year-old, who shuts down whenever anyone tells him he did something wrong and needs to make reparations, clamps so tight we can't see his hurt or his fear or his anger; there are the four-year-olds who care nothing at all for consequences, only care for their curious impulses that lead them to discover what a yard might look like if they emptied the entire recycling container while their mama was doing her workout inside and probably, arguably, should have checked on them but really thought they'd learned their lesson the last time when they had to sit in their seats at the table without playing for an hour because they'd emptied the trash receptacle in the same exact way; and there is the fifteen-month-old who is perfect—at least until he turns three.

All of these children are different. We teach them all the same things, but we do it differently. We have no idea what we're doing. We do what our gut tells us to do. When the nine-year-old comes up with some different point of view about how we should handle bedtime, because he doesn't think he's allowed to stay up late enough, because all his friends get to stay up this late and why can't he, we don't ever know what to do or say the first time (besides the old, maddening, "If your friends were jumping off a cliff..."). We find our way into it.

Sometimes we can put too much pressure on ourselves as parents to know the exact right thing to do in every challenging moment, even though we've never had a moment where we opened a door and the eighteen-month-old is sitting in a room of painted poop—which happened for an excruciating forty days when my twins were eighteen months old.

We can let our not knowing what to do make us feel like

maybe we shouldn't have been parents in the first place. We feel incompetent, broken, not enough—not intelligent enough, patient enough, strategic enough, energetic enough, kind enough, brave enough—for this task before us.

But let me just tell you something: even on the sixth kid, I don't really know what I'm doing. Sure, I know why the baby's crying right now, because I've had a lot of practice in reading cues and being attuned to an infant. I know that right now he's hungry but a few minutes ago he was uncomfortable because he had a wet diaper. And, yes, I know that if I tell the nine-year-old that it's time for bed and he didn't have any kind of advanced warning, he's going to flip out. I know that if I try to forbid the four-year-olds from the LEGO station and the LEGOs are left out, they're not going to have enough impulse control to keep from putting their hands all over their brothers' creations every other minute.

I know that if I tell my seven-year-old he doesn't need another snack, because it's almost time for dinner, he will still find himself wandering over to the refrigerator to see what's inside—not because he's defying the rules but because it's habit; he's always, always hungry. I know that if the six-year-old is asked to find anything, even if it's right in front of his face, it's going to be gone forever and ever and ever and he will need my help to find what's almost touching his head as he lies on the floor and pontificates in a whiny voice about how everything he loves always disappears and why can't he have anything that is just his?

I know all of these things. I know my children. I know

myself. But there are some things that can completely blindside me as a parent. I know that when my sons' school called last year and the nine-year-old (who was then eight) was making threats about hurting himself, I didn't know how to possibly handle it. I know that when the six-year-old told me there was a boy in his class who made fun of him on the playground and liked to knock him down, I didn't know what to do about it. I know that when the seven-year-old said he wanted to play soccer and Husband and I are musicians, writers, and artists, I didn't even have a clue about the first thing I could do.

My kids, after all these years of being a parent, still surprise me. Like the day Twin 1, who was three at the time, took out a bunch of Halloween tattoos someone had given us and decided to put them all over his face so his skin looked like a patterned sheet of ghosts and werewolves and "Happy Halloween" in orange and black. Like the day Twin 2, also three at the time, put on two different shoes, one green and one white, and announced that he was ready to go and then argued for ten minutes about whether or not these shoes belonged together.

Like the afternoon the oldest, eight years old then, stormed up the stairs because he had finished his technology time and he wanted a few more minutes, but, because we're very rigid on how much time our kids spend with technology, the answer was no, and he said in this low, growling voice, "Yooouuuu meeeaaaannnn Dadddddddyyyyyy" and then disappeared from our view, thankfully. Like the morning our third son was only three and announced that duck rhymed with "f*ck" and a bunch of other words we didn't hear because we only heard the one he'd never encountered in his life because no one in our house ever says it. Like the day the second son ate an entire two pounds of grapes while we weren't looking (we didn't even know that was possible. Apparently, his body didn't either, and he was glued to the toilet the rest of the day. Natural consequences.).

Sometimes I don't know whether to laugh or to cry.

There are still times when I feel way in over my head, unsure if I'm the person for this job. Like when the nine-year-old decided to express his anxiety by wrapping a scarf I'd knitted him around his neck and pulling, like he was going to choke himself. Like when the six-year-old scribbled that he hated his brother because he wouldn't let him play. Like when the seven-year-old, who is normally a very encouraging and easy child, said he wished he was in a different family.

Just because I have six children doesn't mean I know what I'm doing all the time, every day. That's okay.

These are the things we learn as we go. We don't have to know everything about parenting when we take our first wobbling steps as a parent. The point of parenting is not to know everything there is to know when we first begin. I read so many parenting books before becoming a parent—I still do! —so I could equip myself with all the knowledge I could possibly gather. Still, I have to find my own way.

We grow, just like our children grow. We make our mistakes, we make our reparations, we make our transformation.

How do we grow? We spend time getting to know our kids

—all their hilarious inconsistencies, their maddening behavioral issues (that make for humorous tales), their dreams and disappointments and hurts and joys. We embrace their fragile, lovely hearts. We love.

And that's always enough.

If a 3-Year-Old Were Giving a State of the Union Address

Dear Mr. Speaker, Mr. Vice President, Members of Congress, my fellow Adult Americans, and, especially, my two parents, sitting over there, shaking their heads:

Today marks the end of the third year I've been alive and the beginning of the year stretching out in front of Birthday Number Four, and let me just tell you, this year is going to be hell. Sorry for the dirty word, Mama and Daddy, but I'm so not joking. Look out, because here I come.

I understand that because this is my third birthday, you'll be going out of your minds over the course of the next year, but I just want to tell you now: I got this. I know everything about everything, so you can stop trying to teach me about the proper way to do things according to you. I know how to do EVERYTHING by myself.

I know how to put on a jacket, even though you said I put it on inside out and upside down, Mama. You don't know what you're talking about. The hood is supposed to be on my booty. Just let me do it. I also know how to put on my shoes, even though you say I put them on the wrong foot. The toes are supposed to point out. That's the way everybody wears them. You obviously don't know anything.

I especially know how to plunge a toilet, so please stop taking the plunger away from me. Trust me. I know what I'm doing. Here. Let me show you.

I hope we can work together this year on pretty much nothing, because I want to be the one who does everything. By myself. (I know I'm repeating myself. But this is an important message. I have to make sure you get it.)

You want to help me into the car? Nope. I will walk back to the place where you started helping me, and I will do it myself. Button my shirt the proper way? I already did! Get your hands away. Help me cross the street safely? Nope. I WILL DO IT MYSELF!

Don't worry. I'll go a little easy on you, at least when you're sleeping. Wait. On second thought, that's probably the time when I will attempt everything I shouldn't do when eyes are watching, because everyone's asleep, and what better time to sneak into the bathroom and drink a whole vial of Peace and Calming essential oil? What better time to steal downstairs and drag the kitchen chair across the floor so I can reach the pan of brownies I saw you put in the microwave for safe-keeping last night? What better time to pick a lock on the front door? You don't even know what I'm capable of. But I'm about to show you. Oh, yes I am.

We are living in a time of extraordinary change—change that is reshaping you but is keeping me the same, because, you know, I'm perfect just the way I am. But you, you need to change, and here are some perfect examples of my point:

You need to stop telling me I need to get in the car, 5, 4, 3, 2, 1, 0. You need to stop telling me the orange plate is actually not clean when it's the only plate I want to use today. And you need to remember that I like the green car grocery cart on Tuesdays and the red car grocery cart on Fridays. I don't know why you can't keep it all straight, because it's the same two colors every week. Except when it's yellow or blue.

So you: change.

Me: stay the same.

We clear on this?

We've been through extraordinary change before. Remember when I first climbed out of my crib, and me and my twin brother would play with our poop and leave you a really nice painting on our walls and clothes and faces? You didn't think you were going to survive that time, did you? And look at you now. You're still alive, I'm still alive, we're all still alive. And I will do greater things yet, and you will survive them, too.

That is, you'll survive them if you let me do what I want, with no repercussions. This is really how kids want to live, you know, and it doesn't matter what their parents say, this is actually the *best* way to live. We just want to do whatever it is we want to do. If we want to take a black Sharpie marker and draw whiskers on our face, let us. If we want to wear our one-year-old brother's pants in the dead of winter, let us. If we want to play with the cars instead of trains, but the trains are already out and scattered everywhere, just let us play with the cars.

Cleaning up is no fun, and we should never have to do it ever again. That's the first law I'd like passed.

Remember: it's my spirit that has made the last three years so fun. You used to say that I had a lot of spirit. Well, my spirit's about to have a growth spurt, because I just figured out that I know how to take the toilet paper roll off the dispenser thingy, and now I will never tire of throwing a brand new toilet paper roll into the toilet and watching it curl at the edges. It always plugs up the toilet when I try to flush down the evidence, but that's perfectly okay. I know how to plunge a toilet, remember?

You face some important choices right now. Will you believe that I know what I'm doing, or will you constantly try to thwart me? I can tell you what I'll do if you constantly try to thwart me. I'll cry at the top of my lungs for half an hour to the tune of "I dinnent have my lunch" so all the people in the park will stare at you. I'll say I hate you and sometimes I'll even hit or kick or bite to punctuate my point, because you parents are unreasonable people. I'll dump out a whole container of shape blocks and I'll throw a car across the room so it dents a wall and I'll slam the door so the walls shake and your favorite picture falls down and breaks.

That's why you should never thwart me. Learn from your mistakes and move on and we'll all be that much happier. Me, especially. Which is all that really matters.

Let's sum this up by talking about some of the problems we have. First, there is you. And then there's you. And then there is…you.

If you could just get out of my way and let me do whatever I want, it would make life so much easier. If you would let me have whatever color plate I want, if you would let me wear whatever I want, if you would let me put my shoes on the right feet (it's not wrong, I'm telling you!), if you would let me unbuckle my five-point harness in the car while we're driving down the highway because I really need to get that pencil I dropped, if you would let me get out of bed whenever I want, if you would let me have any toy I desire, if you would let me play with a billion toys at the same time, your life would be easier, my life would be easier, and we'd all, as a result, be so much happier.

I know this isn't easy. You always say that nothing worth doing is ever easy. You never know what you're going to get when I climb out of bed in the morning. Is it the clever one or the devilish one or the argumentative one or the loving one or the sad one or the angry one or the happy one or the millions of other versions of myself?

But I can promise you that in more than a year, when I am no longer three, you will be so glad that time marches on, because it means I won't stay three forever.

It will get better. I mean, no it won't. Because I'm still here. But I'm clear-eyed and big-hearted and undaunted by challenge. You'll still love me when this year is over.

Thank you. God bless me. God bless me, and God bless… me.

This is Every Family Dinner You've Ever Had

Family dinners are a big deal in my house. Husband, my sons, and I eat dinner together every evening and are usually interrupted once or twice by the neighborhood children, who apparently never eat. Ever.

That aside, we have a grand time sitting around our dinner table and talking about our days. It's raucous and crazy and loud and full of constant chatter—because kids aren't even quiet when they stuff food in their mouths, as hard as their mama tries to teach them manners.

It's probably safe to say that I care a bit more about manners than Husband does, because he doesn't even blink when the kids answer a question with an over-full mouth stuffed with spaghetti, most of which, in their prompt answering, escapes from their mouths to the table, and the rest of which shoots across toward my eyes, since they're laughing so hard at the way that glob looked falling from their mouths. It's about as disgusting as it sounds, so every now and then, you'll hear me sneaking in those reminders: "Don't talk with your mouth full," "Please don't smack," and "Seriously, try not to inhale your food. Chewing is good. And there's plenty."

As much as I love our dinners, I have to admit: I used to envision this nice little quiet family dinner around a table of sweet conversation and delicious food that the kids wouldn't even think of complaining about.

That fantasy left me years ago.

The one thing I can count on when my family sits down to dinner is my kids complaining about what's on the menu before they've even tried it. Doesn't matter if it's mashed potatoes drowned in butter or chicken browned in coconut oil, with a bit of celery seed and thyme sprinkled on top or (their favorite) sautéed asparagus, they're going to complain. If I believed them, my kids wouldn't like hamburgers, chicken soup, grilled cheese, breakfast for dinner or, especially, carrot chips.

It never fails that a kid will come traipsing into the house, after playing outside with his friends and working up an appetite as only boys can do, and he will sniff the air and say, "Something smells yummy," after which he will walk over to the stove, and, upon seeing what's cooking, say, "Aw, man. I don't like that," to which I will reply, "Welp. More for me."

Once they taste what's for dinner, there's not really a problem, but those few minutes between dinner showing up and kids shoveling it in their mouths are quite a problem for now. If I thought blindfolds would work to combat the complaining, I'd invest in half a dozen. But then they'd probably just complain about the smells.

When we're all seated at the table, with our plates full, at least three of my sons will ask to be excused so they can get some milk. It's not a problem at all; they asked the correct way, so of course we say yes. They pour their milk and bring it back to the table, and thirty seconds later it's all over the floor and my legs.

This happens just about every night. It doesn't matter how long they've been practicing drinking milk in a cup, someone is going to spill. You might wonder why this happens with such amazing consistency. Well, we are eight people crammed at a table built for four. A new kitchen table is not in our budget, so we sit practically on top of each other. Every now and then our boys will ask why we can't use the dining room table, which was built for at least six people. We give some excuse about how it's a glass table and we don't feel like cleaning up all the fingerprints boys will paint on it when they use its underside as a napkin, even though they have a perfectly efficient cloth one spread out on their lap. I'd rather not know what happens underneath a table, and a glass table leaves nothing to the imagination.

There is also such thing as a Thermos, which would eliminate the possibility of those frequent spills. But let me tell you what happens to Thermoses in our world.

1. Boy pours milk.
2. Boy puts lid on Thermos.
3. Boy drinks most of the milk, but not all.
4. Boy loses the Thermos somewhere between end-of-dinner and after-dinner chores.
5. Parents find missing Thermos six weeks later.

6. No one wants to open it.

I'll take milk spills over curdled milk any day.

Next on the list for the perfect family dinner is an inability to remain at the table. My boys remember to ask to be excused about once out of four times. It's still a mystery to me how they're sitting there eating a bowl of spaghetti squash, and they suddenly remember this flower drawing they did in art class today, and they have to show me right now or they're going to die. Or, two minutes after dinner begins, they realize they need to go potty. Or, ten minutes after dinner begins, one of their friends rings the doorbell, because they apparently think we can eat dinner in ten minutes.

They get up to see what their brother laughed out his nose. They get up to grab the food they dropped on the floor. They get up just to get up.

When they finally sit down long enough to actually have a conversation, everybody's yelling. This happens because the boys are trying to tell Husband and me about their days, and no one's taking turns with the talking, so they think if they just talk louder maybe they'll have a better chance of getting heard.

This is the time in our dinner when I usually reach my system overload and start talking like a robot, repeating the words, "System overload. System overload. System overload." until everyone looks at me like I'm crazy. It works. The table grows silent, everyone wondering how close Mama is to meltdown mode (no one wants to see that again). And because of this, we can finally take turns asking each of them about their days and get a portion of the story before one brother interrupts another with something they forgot to say during their turn. It doesn't take long for the talking to turn back into yelling, but by then there's no more food left anyway. Dinner's over.

At some point during the dinner, someone will make a potty joke. This is one other characteristic of dinner I can always count on. Someone will fart and send the whole table into peals of laughter and then "Oh my gosh, it smells so bad" proclamations. Someone will burp and crack everybody up again. Someone will arm fart "The Star-Spangled Banner" while the rest of us watch, mesmerized. Someone will tell a joke that contains the words, "poop," "pee" and "armpits" in the same sentence. They think it's the most hilarious thing in the world, and sometimes I do, too—until they start talking about vomit.

That's when I like to say, "We're eating, guys. Please don't mess up this broccoli cauliflower cheese soup for me." Because, you know, it wasn't hard enough to get them to eat it in the first place. Now every time they look at it, they'll see chartreuse vomit. Challenge accepted.

Whoever has the sweeping chore for the week always has quite a job to look forward to after dinner. This is mostly due to the fourteen-month-old, who has a proficient mastery of identifying the color green and eliminating it from his tray. But the four-year-olds aren't all that great either. They attempt to stuff green beans into the cave between their booster seats and the chair those boosters are sitting on, except they aren't great at aiming, so that hideaway food ends up in a pile under the table. We don't have a dog, so all this food—which could probably feed a small country—mostly goes to waste. It really is a shame.

Every night, when we finish dinner, I find myself wondering whether I actually live with a pack of raccoons disguised as good-looking little boys. I'm just glad I don't have to sweep the floor anymore.

And the last thing I can always count on, no matter the day or what's for dinner or how much we had to eat, is my four-year-old twins saying they're still hungry—because three bowls of chicken noodle soup were not enough for a forty-pound kid. They will eat their body weight in pizza and still say they're hungry when it's all said and done.

All in all, even with the noisy, disgusting, messy displays of my children, family dinners are my favorite part of the day. Mostly because I enjoy eating. But also because I enjoy sitting together, laughing together, and talking together about whatever it is that makes my boys laugh or cry or smile or scowl or feel glad to be a part of this wacky family.

And those nights when they end dinner saying, "This was the best dinner ever!"? I call that winning.

Hasn't happened yet. But I'm sure it's right around the corner.

The Memory Banks of Children: a Modern Mystery

Kids have the most amazing memory banks. I've never actually been able to figure them out, only marvel at them.

My ten-year-old will forget to put his empty bowl in the sink five seconds after I remind him, but he will miraculously remember that, two weeks ago, his daddy and I mentioned he'd be able to have a little bit more technology time on his brother's birthday. He will forget his homework on the chair where I set it while repeating the words, "Don't forget your homework," but he will remember that a month ago Husband told him he could start a YouTube channel after school today.

He will remember what we whispered in our bedroom while the door was closed—that he might get another chance with the tech time he lost yesterday (he has an amazing ability to hear when it suits him)—and will forget to pack up his blue folder in his backpack on school mornings, even though he's done it—or been expected to do it—for four years now. He will remember that we said we'd reward him for doing specific jobs around the house that are not considered typical chores, but he will forget that we agreed to take money away for every article of clothing he leaves on the floor, which means he has a negative balance this month. When we remind him of this latter reality, people in Paris will be able to hear his, "What?!!"

My twins will remember the one day we stopped by Dominoes after church and decided to buy lunch instead of fix it, but they will not remember the thousands of other times we drove by this same Dominoes and only had peanut butter and jelly sandwiches (and other healthy choices) for lunch. My seven-year-old will remember where he saw me hide that stash of treats that's only supposed to be consumed by the adults in the house after the kids have gone to bed, but he'll forget where he's supposed to put his jacket, his shoes, and his underwear when he takes them off for a bath (actually, hold the underwear; he forgot to wear them today). The six-year-old will remember what I told him we were going to have for dinner tonight (breakfast for dinner), even though I no longer feel like cooking that meal anymore, but he will not remember what he needs to do after dinner (stay in the kitchen and do his chore).

It's astounding to me both how much children can remember and how much they forget. They remember that one time I totally lost it because someone was making The Most Annoying Noise in the World (which, if you haven't had the great privilege of hearing it, is a cross between a scream, a whine, and a cry), but they will forget the hundreds of other times I have spoken softly and calmly during their meltdowns.

My oldest enforces the rules that we have in our home with great regularity and has no trouble pointing out when one of his brothers is breaking them, but there is a giant plank in his eye when it comes to breaking the rules himself. "I didn't know that was a rule," he says with all the feigned innocence he can muster, after being gently reminded that arm farts are not allowed at the table—even though, right before he got in trouble for doing it, he'd pointed out that one of his brothers was arm-farting "The Star-Spangled Banner," and that wasn't allowed.

What I have learned about the memory banks of children is that there is only enough room in those banks for whatever is convenient for the individual child. This means that if they don't want to remember the rule that says the only thing they do with their almost-bedtime window is read, they won't. They have selective memory that says they can only, logically, hold within their minds what most benefits them. This is why a kid will remember that you bought some treats at the store today, but he will not remember what he did earlier today that now renders him ineligible for the treat.

As for me, I can't even remember the things that benefit me—my name (Mama), when I'm supposed to have a day off (never), where I put those chocolates Husband brought home from the store the other day (I've looked everywhere).

Kids are inconsistent beings who sometimes forget the most impressive and illogical of things, but at least when I step out of line (like, say, forget I told them yesterday that they could have a friend over today, even though I have a massive headache), they jump at the chance to keep me honest and consistent.

You don't even really need a memory bank when you have kids.

Inventions that Would Help Parents Make it Through the Day

There are some great inventions out on the market today that have made my life easier. We don't always have the funds to invest in something new and spectacular, but when we do, watch out. A crockpot? Yep, made life easier *and* my kids actually get dinner now (there is a Before Crockpot life and an After Crockpot life, one clearly better than the other). The Internet? Hey, that's Husband's livelihood, so I sure am glad for it. An app for tracking my last period? I don't know who I'd be without it.

But there are still some gaping holes in the make-life-easier department, especially when it comes to parents. I would like the inventors to get on these ASAP (and you're welcome for the ideas).

1. A divider glass between the front seat and the back seat(s) of every vehicle.

I own a minivan. It's the only vehicle large enough to hold my six kids, but it is not a vehicle large enough to make ignoring them even a remote possibility. Every time we load up to take a trip, even if it's to the grocery store ten minutes down the road, the first question Husband and I hear, before we even pull out of our drive, is "Are we almost there?"

If we happen to be traveling farther than fifteen minutes down the road, we're in for a very long trip with billions of opportunities to exercise our patience. I'm tired, I'm hungry, I'm bored, my back hurts, I dropped my pencil, you made my book fall, he hit me, he's copying me, he's laying on me, he's touching me, he's looking at me, are we almost there, are we almost there, are we almost there?

I don't want billions of opportunities to exercise my patience. I would like a transparent, durable divider between my seat and theirs so that when things get out of hand, all I have to do is touch a button, wave in the rearview, and say, "You're on your own now, kids. See you in a few."

2. A comfortable cone of silence to put over my face.

This would, of course, have to be a really strong cone of silence. My kids speak at an average of three thousand decibels. I am an introvert who, by dinnertime, has had it with the noise six boys can create.

I would slip on this cone of silence when my kids are losing their minds about is dinner ready they're really hungry they're starving I'm such a mean mom I won't let them have a snack two minutes before dinner (they've already had four). I would use this cone of silence when my nine-year-old starts talking about Pokémon or Minecraft. I would hide beneath it when my twins figure out another way to scale the wall and get to their clothes in the closet so they don't hear what I have to say about how their closet is now, for the twelfth time this week, all over their floor.

I have no expectation for what this cone looks like. It could look like a giant black spider for all I care (I'd make that sacrifice). In fact, that might be better. Then I'll have extra protection, because my sons would be too afraid to venture near.

3. An invisibility cloak.

This cloak would be used for those moments that require stealth, such as when the baby is down and ready to go to sleep, even closing his eyes, but the moment I try to silently slide by his room on my way downstairs to retrieve the book I left there, he's suddenly wide awake and I'll have to pick him up and rock him to sleep all over again (as if I mind. I really don't. But the cloak would come in handy.).

An invisibility cloak would have multiple purposes. It could also be helpful when Husband is trying to smuggle restaurant food into our bedroom when our kids are already supposed to be asleep (there would be an extra feature on this cloak to neutralize the smell of chips and queso and the fried chicken sandwich). It would also help a parent successfully sneak out of the house for a minute to themselves without someone following them, asking for something—like another orange or the answer to one hundred forty-seven times eighty-nine (as if I have enough brain cells to complete that in my head) or the miracle of turning back time cloaked as, "Just one more chance. Please?"

4. Toilet paper dispensers that have a lock and a key.

An invention like this would save me considerable money.

My three-year-old twins, you see, are really, really good at experiments like, "What happens when you throw a whole roll of toilet paper in the toilet I just peed in?" They do it about every other day. They think it's funny to watch the edges of the toilet paper curl and the way white caves in on itself.

It's not funny. These experiments cost me at least fifteen dollars a month. For the mathematically impaired, that's one hundred eighty dollars a year. That would pay for my electricity bill any month that's not part of a Texas summer (there aren't many).

I would like a toilet paper dispenser that's not afraid to stand up against three-year-old hands, please.

5. A magic pill that makes a kid feel full.

Boys are something else. They can eat a whole pound of strawberries, and they're still hungry. They can eat twelve bananas in one sitting, and they're still hungry. They can stuff an entire loaf of bread in their mouths, along with a stick of butter, and they will still be hungry.

A pill that could tell them they're actually just bored would be fantastic. My grocery bill will thank you.

6. A mobile shoe-tracking app.

I would love to download an app onto my phone that would tell me where every right shoe the five-year-old owns is hiding, because this is getting a little ridiculous. He wasn't born with two left feet, but looking at his shoe basket, you would think someone thought it would be funny to put us in an episode of Punk'd called "Where Did All the Right Shoes Go?"

Every morning my five-year-old is supposed to get ready

for school, which includes putting on shoes. And every morning it's the same old story: Two left shoes where yesterday there was a right and a left.

I have spent hours of my life looking for shoes only so they can promptly become lost again. An shoe-tracking app could literally add hours to my life.

I would try to invent these products myself, but the only things I've ever been good at inventing are stories. Plus, my mind has never been the same since having children.

I guess that could explain why all these nonexistent inventions seem so utterly brilliant.

HILLS I'M NOT WILLING TO LIE DOWN ON

A Dad is Not a Babysitter or a Helper; He's a Parent

You know what would be nice? It would be nice to live in a world where men didn't get pushed up on a pedestal for "helping" take care of their children. It would be nice to live in a world where men take care of their children and it's not considered exceptionally exceptional.

I get it. We live in a world that is still finding its way into gender equality, that is still fighting for equal rights for women in the workplace, because, go figure, some women choose to have a career outside of babies and children and home. We are still figuring all this out. Traditionally, men were the breadwinners and women the caretakers, and that meant men didn't do such things as "taking care of the kids." So this is a new-ish thing for us. But I feel like maybe we should be farther along than we are.

Husband and I are very happily married. But, during prime working hours—6 a.m. to 5:30 p.m.—we split our parenting duties as if we're single parents. Weekends and evenings we hang out together as a family, of course, but on the weekdays it's one parent on six. I take the morning shift, cooking breakfast, fixing lunches, making sure kids brush their teeth and dress in appropriate clothing and get their shoes, walking them all to school, walking the three who aren't in school back home, keeping twins out of mud and toilets, entertaining the baby, reading them stories, putting them all down for naps.

Husband takes over at 12:30 p.m., while they're sleeping. They sleep until 3, after which time he wrestles with them and sends them outside to play and invites their friends over to play so there are twelve or thirteen kids in the house (my anxiety just went through the roof) and makes them do their homework. He knows where all the kids' school papers go, and he signs all their reading logs and marks their behavior folders and makes sure their lunch stuff gets put in the sink and washed for tomorrow. He feeds the baby and changes diapers and makes kids clean up their toys before dinner so the house is somewhat tidy by the time the day is through, and then he cooks dinner.

This is not exceptional. This is called Being a Parent.

People are shocked that we do it this way. "Must be nice to have a husband who helps like that," they say.

Well, I wasn't the only one who decided to have six kids. I was not the only participant, either. Of course he's gonna help so I can work, too.

See, what my husband understands (and I guess this is where he'd be exceptional—because it seems there aren't many who understand it) is that I am a better mother because of my work. Not everyone is. That's okay. I am. He gets that, and he's happy to make sure I get to pursue a career.

But when he's watching the kids so I can hole up in my room and write a handful of essays and stories that may change lives, it's not babysitting. When I go out once a month with my book club friends to talk about a book for all of five minutes and then talk about our lives for another three hours, that's not babysitting. When he decides to bake some chicken in the oven or organize some out-of-control papers or take the baby for a few hours while I get a little extra sleep, he's not just "helping." He's parenting.

Friends and babysitters and full-time nannies help. Dads parent.

I'm glad we could set that straight.

A Dad Knows What He's Doing. We Should Let Him Do It.

We've now established that a dad is not a babysitter because he's a parent. There is a logical next step to this equation, and it looks like this:

A parent knows what he's doing.

It seems that not only have we, as a society, gotten so used to seeing Mom as the sole caretaker of her children that we scarcely question it anymore, but we have also, as a result, gotten used to believing the myth that Dad is an incompetent caretaker.

We see this myth everywhere. We see it in the public men's restrooms that have no changing station included, because men, of course, would not know how to change a diaper if their kid's diaper exploded in their face. We see it in the lack of paternity leave at most businesses (maternity leave's not much better, but that's another subject for another day), as if no father in his right mind would want to spend those early weeks helping his partner and acclimating himself to this new dynamic of family. We see it in our television shows and our movies and our commentary on clueless celebrity dads who carry their children all wrong in slings (who among us really knows what we're doing the first time out of the gate, anyway?).

Maybe this is where the root of the real problem lies, why both women *and* men express outrage at seeing men put on pedestals for taking responsibility as a parent. The truth is, most men don't want that pedestal any more than women do. Most dads don't want to be held up as an exception when they're just loving their kids the best way they know how—some days that means taking care of the explosion that happened in their six-month-old's pants, and some days it means mopping up the puke coloring the carpet in the hall, and some days it means teaching a kid how to ride a bike or roller blade or drive.

Of course we want to thank dads for their contribution to raising their kids. Of course we want to acknowledge that they're doing a great job as a parent, same as mothers are. Of course we want to make sure they know how beautiful it is to see a dad loving their kids with his time.

But what our "Dad's babysitting tonight" does is it unconsciously undermines who men are as parents. Babysitters don't know their children. Babysitters aren't obligated to stick around. Babysitters don't make decisions about what to do with the kid who's getting beat up in school or how to handle the not-turning-in-homework conundrum or where to put the baby until he's sleeping through the night.

Husband and I parent differently. Our sons know what to expect when each parent takes over the parenting watch. They know that I don't like a lot of noise, so if they want to wrestle or play freeze tag, they better do it out back. They know their daddy doesn't care about noise as much as I do, so they can play music through the loudspeakers and try to talk over that music if they so desire. They know their daddy lets them read stories in the home library while I prefer they read in the living room with me. They know they can probably get away with some things when Husband's on duty that I would never tolerate and vice versa. We have different preferences because we're different people. Our kids adjust accordingly.

But just because we do things differently doesn't mean I'm a better parent than he is. It doesn't mean he has no idea what he's doing.

It seems that we've traveled a little too far down this path of Dad as the joke, Dad as little more than useless, Dad as a bungling idiot. It's time to change this perception, too.

I know men who don't have sole custody of their kids, and they want nothing more than to be less of a babysitter, as mandated by courts, and more of a dad. I know men who stay home while their wives work full time, and they want nothing more than to be seen as competent caregivers who have access to changing tables when out shopping for groceries. I know men who are as serious about their parenting as they are about their weight-lifting, and they want nothing more than to be seen as responsible, involved, loving dads.

Dads know what they're doing. We should let them do it.

The Imaginary Lives of Perfect Parents

Everywhere I look—at least on the Internet—I see perfect parenting. There is proof of perfect parents on parenting blogs, forums, social media threads, anything that shines a light on the brilliance that is a parent who never fails to discipline, never wants to give up, never needs help, and always approaches their responsibility with perfect patience, perfect follow-through, perfect methodology.

On the other side of this spectrum, there is me.

I've been called an abomination to motherhood; an inexperienced, ugly mother of future criminals; and a helicopter parent, a permissive parent, a controlling parent, a no-control parent, a too-structured parent, a lackadaisical parent, a cares-too-little parent, and a cares-too-much parent (I should get an award for achieving every polar opposite there is in the parenting world). I've been told it's a shame I have so many children to release into society when I am clearly so ridiculously inept at this motherhood thing. I've been told I should suck it up, get off my backside, and do society a favor so my kids are actually decent human beings.

People are astonishingly kind nowadays.

The Perfect Parents Club is a relatively difficult club to join. It doesn't have any dues, but it does have some requirements, which include but are not limited to the following:

1. Memory loss.

When Perfect Parents say something like, "My kid never did anything like that," you can rest assured that they are most likely suffering from memory loss. There is not a child on the planet who has not ever thrown some kind of temper tantrum (however wild or mild it may be), because every child has a mind of his or her own, and at some point in time, what a parent wants is going to come into direct conflict with what a child wants. It's the thrill and magic of being human, of being completely different people with different ideas and different expectations. If a kid never talked back or asserted himself or herself, then there are bigger problems at stake. It means a kid is either afraid to state his or her opinions or they are so effectively brainwashed that they have no opinion at all.

I'd rather take the alternative: a kid who knows who he is and what he wants.

Fortunately, most parents who say "my kid never did that" are usually only suffering from a simple, reversible case of Memory Loss.

2. Denial.

Perfect Parents also must have a good grasp on denial when they read a story about a parent whose daughter refused to wear a certain color because of some inane reason known only to three-year-olds, because this is the exact right time when they must declare, with full conviction: "I would never have allowed my child to do that." In this case, it's not that our Perfect Parent has forgotten all the nonsensical things their kid ever did or said; it's that their memories have been overlaid with a good film of Denial.

They never would have let their kid dance in rain puddles when they were instructed not to dance in rain puddles, they never would have turned the other cheek when their kid snuck an extra carrot or two for snack time, they never would have carried a boneless kid home from a park—they would have made that boneless kid walk.

A healthy sense of denial helps Perfect Parents reframe memories with better memories of kids who did what they were told all the time, never sassed, and never embarrassed them in front of other people. In other words, with a good dose of denial, real kids can become Perfect Kids.

3. A loud voice of judgment.

Perfect Parents like to weigh in on things like discipline and boundaries because they've forgotten that every child is different and they believe, since their child was perfect thanks to faulty memories and denial filters, that every kid who doesn't behave perfectly must be the product of bad parenting. Our morals are failing. Our discipline is lax. Our world is going up in smoke; have you seen the kids of today?

They express this opinion loudly, every opportunity they have, making sure they point back to their perfect parenting abilities. Which leads me to:

4. An inflated sense of parenting abilities.

Perfect Parents mistakenly believe that the reason their children behave or behaved perfectly (at least in their memories) is because of their stellar parenting abilities. Some people have it, some people don't. Whatever. The ones who complain about their kids' behavior problems—or who, in my case, make fun of them; even worse!—should step up their parenting game.

Perfect Parents are more than happy to tell other parents how they should raise their kids, because they clearly have it all figured out; they're doing everything exactly right.

They forget that children are people and that some parts of this behavior game are just the luck of the draw. I have six kids. Four of them argue about everything—and I mean, literally, everything. Two of them do everything we ask. We are the same parents to all. I'll let you figure that one out on your own, Perfect Parents, but here's a little hint: It has more to do with the kids than you'd like to admit.

5. Unconsciousness.

One thing that could be said for all of us is that we are all Perfect Parents—when we're unconscious. I'm a Perfect Parent between the hours of 9 p.m. and 4:15 a.m., otherwise known as the hours I'm sleeping. Unless, of course, one of them wakes up.

Before I had kids, I thought I might have a slim shot at being a Perfect Parent, but my first kid was a creative and gifted one. The second was a compliant social one, the third was hard-headed, and the fourth and fifth were twins. Any notion of perfect parenting flew out the window the first time my creative son, at two, negotiated his first contract for a small business.

And now, so that I will never forget how imperfect my parenting was and is, I keep detailed records.

Perfect Parents are a figment of the imagination. The rest of us—the imperfect ones—can all rest easy.

After all, I'd rather be real than imaginary.

How to Become a Sisterhood of Mothers

My younger sister is about to celebrate her birthday, so lately I've been thinking about all the things I love about her. I know not everyone has a good relationship with their sister, but I consider my sister one of my best friends. She knows everything about me. She can tell what I'm thinking before I say a word. The day she left me alone with my firstborn son, she knew how terrified I was just by looking into my thought-I-was-hiding-it-well face, and I'll never forget her hug and that gentle, "You're gonna be all right" for all the days of my life, because in one moment, she gave me the courage to be a mom.

My sister is kind and loving and faithful and never forgets to call on one of my kids' birthdays even though I forget to call on hers. She loves her family, loves her nephews, understands that we are never going to be perfect at this family thing or this parenting thing or this growing up thing. She gets me. And I'm pretty sure she appreciates me almost as much as I appreciate her.

That's all well and good; I get along with my own blood-related sister. The question is: How well do I get along with all my not-blood-related sisters?

I get so tired of the fights, honestly. It's wearying like nothing else (except a kid who whines all day. That's the best rival for parenting fights.). I don't feel half as tired from wrestling my six boys through a day as I do from all the parenting wars that pit sister against sister and hand out wounded hearts like they make not a difference in the world.

They do make a difference.

We are all sisters, from the very beginning. And then we have children, and our sisterhood becomes something great (or it should). Sure, we do our parenting in different ways. My sister breastfeeds. I didn't, because I could never get enough milk out to keep my babies from emergency rooms (and I tried). She's never used cloth diapers. I used them for half my children before twins burned us out.

Some of us let our kids sleep with us. I've never let our babies sleep with us, unless they woke at four in the morning and I needed another hour of sleep. Some of us hover on playgrounds, and some of us keep to the perimeters, with eyes on our children but hands off. Some of us have perfectly compliant children, and some of us have fighters who will fight about every little thing, at least until they learn that it's possible —and more effective—to choose their battles.

Some of us have one kid, some of us have six, some of us let our kids help make decisions, some of us would never let a kid make a decision if our life depended on it, some of us make our kids do chores, some of us don't, some of us let our kids watch television and play on screens to their hearts' content, and some of us limit tech time.

Some of us have three kids smashed into one room, some of us believe every kid needs his own room, some of us are saving for college, some of us haven't even thought about it, some of us let our kids cuss, some of us wouldn't think of allowing it, some of us take our kids to counseling, some of us want to make sure we can handle this on our own, some of us send our kids to daycare, some of us stay home with them, some of us enroll our kids in public school, some of us run a homeschool operation, some of us pick up our kids every time they cry, some of us let them cry it out sometimes, some of us would give anything in the world to be home with our kids, some of us find great fulfillment in our work and motherhood didn't change that.

The list goes on and on and on. The point is, we're all different. That doesn't mean we're wrong.

See, the thing about a sisterhood is that we are as different as our faces and our bodies and the shape that our lives have taken around our children. We'll never be the same. And yet we *are* the same.

It sounds like a paradox, but it's not really. We all come in different shapes and sizes and colors, and we all come from different backgrounds and beliefs and socioeconomic situations, which means that our philosophies and our choices and our reasons behind those choices will never be exactly the same. But our underneaths are the same. We're all mothers trying to do the best we can for these little irrational human beings who know how to push our buttons, who some days cling to us like our childhood nickname and other days can't stand the sight of us, who wake up different people every day so we have to constantly be on our toes.

We're all doing the best we can.

What I'm most definitely not saying by doing something differently than you do is that you're wrong. This, I think, is where the root of the problem lies. So I'll say it again.

Just because I do something differently than you do it, I'm not saying you're wrong—because I understand that your kid is not my kid and my kid is not your kid, and people who don't spend twenty-four hours seven days a week with my kid don't understand that when you have two three-year-old twins who like to roam at night while everyone else is sleeping so they can ingest a whole tube of toothpaste or a whole bottle of vitamins they somehow pried open, even though I break a nail every time I try, you have to turn a doorknob around so it locks from the outside, or else you might wake up to the whole house burning down around you.

People who don't spent twenty-four hours seven days a week with my kid don't understand that working through a tantrum with the boy prone to anxiety and depression is, in the long run, way better than punishing him for something he's done. People who don't spend twenty-four hours seven days a week with my kid don't understand that technology turns the easiest five-year-old into the Whine Monster, so it's banished from our house, for now.

You don't know my kid. I don't know yours. I can't parent yours. You can't parent mine.

So maybe we should stop trying.

Our differences are what make us beautiful. And what makes us a sisterhood is accepting each other, as is, and putting aside all the differences to acknowledge that this raising a kid thing? It's not easy. We need each other to do it.

We're all doing the best we can. And that is always, always enough.

Should Kids Be Allowed in All Restaurants?

I'm no stranger to the kids-in-restaurants debate. It's been going on for a while, and I always like to keep tabs on it, because I feel pretty strongly about my own point of view. I've stayed silent mostly, because I'm more of a peacemaker than a troublemaker. I'm not a confrontational person by nature, and I'll cry if you look at me wrong.

But there are some things that are worth being said.

There are restaurants that have actually banned children from entering their doors. Which means, in essence, that parents have been—not all the time, but some of the time—banned as well, since parents can't always get away without their children.

There is also an abundance of people who will make parents feel so miserable when they're out to eat that families will resolve to never go to that restaurant again, at least if they must bring their kids. There are people who don't understand—because they've never had children—or don't remember what it's like to take children out to eat and why it's valuable.

I get it, sort of. When a kid's being loud and obnoxious, it can be a huge distraction for someone who's trying to carry on a conversation with his or her partner. Husband and I get a taste of this every evening around our own dinner table.

But the thing is, how will children ever learn how to behave in a restaurant if they never get to go to a restaurant in the first place?

Husband and I don't take our kids out to eat often, and it's not because of the stares or because we think we'll make the other diners uncomfortable. I could care less about that sort of thing. It's more about the size of that restaurant bill after feeding six kids who are boys. It's not pretty.

But, on occasion, we do take our kids out for a nice little treat. Usually it's for a special occasion, like a birthday fun day, where we've spent all day out at the city zoo or a children's museum or walking the downtown streets of the great city of San Antonio visiting the old historical sites. So by the time we get to the eating out part of this Family Fun Day, my kids are not only hungry but they're also exhausted. And we've had a little too much family togetherness.

My sons are very well behaved in restaurants. But they didn't get there overnight. They got that way through the amazing tool called Practice.

My sons, like any other person, deserve to sit down to a meal that's not like the meals they eat in our home every day—we're health food junkies—because they turned seven today or they read a million words for Accelerated Reader or they got into a gifted-and-talented program or they learned to ride a bike without training wheels or they just accomplished fourteen days clean and dry. They should be able to celebrate without feeling the condemning looks of other people who think they should be someone different, someone better, someone quieter and less noticeable.

I understand that you've paid for your fancy (or not-so-fancy) dinner, and you don't want to hear a kid screaming in the middle of your meal (if mine were screaming, I'd take him outside for a little talk), but I don't need someone else telling me what I should and should not do with my children. We've got a little too much of that going on in our world already.

When I take my kids out to restaurants, they get to experience what it's like to eat in a place other than their table at home, and they get to learn proper manners in a public setting, and they get to observe the ways that other people conduct their meals and be glad that we don't allow phones at our table. (If I were you, I'd ban phones from restaurants, not children.)

I remember back when Husband and I only had a toddler and a newborn infant, and one night we decided to go out to eat, because I was getting cabin fever cooped up in the house all day. There was a white-haired couple who came in to the restaurant, and when the waitress asked if the booth beside ours was okay, they took a good long look at us, and I thought, for a minute, that they might say no, they wanted to sit anywhere but beside us. But then the woman beamed at me, turned to the waitress, and said, "Yes, of course." She put down her purse, promptly perched on the edge of her booth, and exclaimed over the new baby. For the next fifteen minutes, this man and woman told me what they remembered from their sons' early days. At one point, the woman patted my hand and said, "It gets easier. It really does."

When our food arrived, she and her husband turned back to their own table. When our check came, it had already been paid.

I wonder how the world might be different if we all had such welcoming, understanding hearts?

A Day in the Life of a Mom

Wake up, wake up, it's time to start the day, come down to breakfast, don't play around now, put that book down, get downstairs, make sure you don't forget socks with your shoes, put your shoes on, you should tie your laces so you don't trip over them, where are your shoes? I have no idea where they are, did you leave them outside? You probably left them outside, go look, they're all wet? Well, you'll still have to wear them because you don't have any others, pack up your backpack, we're leaving in ten minutes, pack up your backpack, we're leaving in five minutes, get your backpack, one more minute, well, looks like you're walking yourself to school, because your brothers and I are leaving, remember, if you're late to school that means you don't get technology time when you get home, come on, boys, stay out of the street, keep close to me, on the grass, make sure you don't get your shoes too terribly wet, watch out for that sprinkler, oh, watch out for the dog poop, please don't step in the dog poop, welp, now we're gonna have to clean your shoes off, come over here, wait boys, we have to clean the poop off so your brother doesn't track it inside the school, don't cross the street yet, you need to wait for me, there are cars coming, okay, ready, set, go! You're getting too far ahead, wait up for us, watch where you're going, share the sidewalk, don't stop when you're walking right in front of me, hurry up, we can't be late for school, hold the door, please, wait for me, let's be quiet through the hallways, don't stand on the bench, let's walk your brothers to their classes, I love you, remember who you are—strong, kind, courageous, and mostly son, have a wonderful day, okay, come on, boys, let's go back home, are you cold? Let's fix your jacket, hold the door open, please, see you later, Ms. Martinez, slow down, boys, stop before you get to the street, do not cross without me, I'm coming as fast as I can, this stroller isn't a running one, wait a minute, let me get a picture of you with that flower, okay, let's cross, one more street, we can do it, I know you're tired, I know it's cold, yay! we're home, what do you want to play with? Please stay out of that, stay out of that, stay out of that, for the love, please leave things alone, just leave it alone, you know what you can play with and what you should leave alone, okay, thank God, it's story time, go pick some stories, let's read, time for naps, better stay in your beds, I'll be right here, [go to work], someone's knocking, it's time for dinner, don't race down the stairs, I'm coming, I'm coming, everybody's here, let's pray, what was the best part of your day, everybody listen, your brother's trying to talk, be quiet, hey, your brother is trying to talk and it's not polite to interrupt, this is a really great dinner, thank you Daddy, how could you possibly still be hungry, you've had three plates, make sure you eat all your vegetables, they're good for you, don't eat too much, though, your tummy will hurt, don't put your elbows on the table, keep your voices down, please, wait, guys, wait, where did you go, it's time for after-dinner chores, don't hit your brother, make sure you put your shoes where they belong so you can find them tomorrow, don't go out front without a parent watching, how many times do I have to tell you, doesn't matter if you're a big boy, you have no idea how to stay alive without a parent watching, hey, don't hurt your brother just because you feel angry, remember: we don't hurt people in our anger, we use our words to express how we feel, time for baths, time to get out, I said put the toys down and get out of the bath, let's read some stories, everybody be quiet, I can't read over your voices and I really don't like to try, be quiet, hey guys, be quiet, get off me, I don't mind when you sit in my lap but when you start wrestling you're gone, stop touching me, stop touching me, *stop touching me*, okay silent reading time, I said silent reading time, does anybody know what silent means? apparently I'm the only one, you know what, everybody just brush your teeth and get in bed, I said it's time for bed, get back in your bed, get.back.in.your.bed., GET BACK IN YOUR BED, get back in your bed get back in your bed get back in your bed…

Husband: Want to…?

Me: Nope.

How to Make a Little Girl Question Her Worth

Every month I sit with a group of ladies and discuss the book of the month and, mostly, our lives. We eat chocolate and drink a little wine and sort through all the things that have happened to us in the stretch between the last meeting and this one.

At the most recent meeting, we found ourselves talking about beauty and body image (because we're women, and this is a big deal to women).

One of my friends is an elementary school teacher. Something disturbing had recently happened at her school. Some first-grade girls were playing on the playground and, because they all took gymnastics, they decided to start a gymnastics club. Another little girl, who did not take gymnastics, wanted to be in their club, too. When she asked permission, however, one of the gymnasts (who is only six or seven, keep in mind) told her, "You have to be skinny to be in the gymnastics club."

She didn't say this in a mean way or a judgmental way or a meant-to-be-hurtful way. She said it matter-of-factly, repeating something she'd likely been told or something she'd overheard.

So the other little girl, who was not allowed entry into this playground gymnastics club, went home and asked her mom, who is thin, if her mom could help her be thinner. This little girl is not fat. She's simply rounder, as many six- and seven-year-olds who have not yet grown into their bodies are. Her mom took the problem to the school, trying to figure out why her daughter, who was way too young to be aware of body image, had come home asking how she could make herself thinner.

The little girls don't know any better. But the adults in their lives do.

And we should be doing better.

Do you know what a little girl hears when she is six years old and can't be in some stupid club because she's not thin enough? She will hear for the rest of her life that she is not thin enough to be in some ridiculous exclusive club.

I know. I was once that little girl.

See, when I was six years old, my parents didn't have a whole lot of money. But they scrimped up enough to put me in a ballet class—at least before they divorced and my dad was gone. I was a tall girl, awkward—big-boned, my mother called me. When I look back at the pictures of me as a child, I was not a fat little girl, but I was built a little larger than others.

After I had been taking ballet lessons for a couple of months, my mom and the ballet instructor had a quiet talk, during which (I was listening in the doorway, as I had learned to do if I ever wanted to hear important things) the instructor, who had a French accent if my memory is correct, told my mother that I was probably going to be too "large" for ballet and my mom shouldn't waste her money. She said it matter-of-factly, as though there was no room for argument.

Now. I understand that there are certain body types that will do well with the rigors demanded by ballet, and there are certain body types that make the mechanics of gymnastics easier. But if we are urging our six-year-olds to concern themselves with being thinner just so they can achieve that body type and somehow have some kind of leg up on all the others, then we're going about it all wrong (fortunately, my mother never took me back to that class, though the words stuck with me for a very long time).

Girls that young should not even be aware of their bodies and what's wrong with them. We have plenty of time for that awakening later (and the world will make sure we experience The Awakening). Girls that young should be playing out on school playgrounds, enjoying the company of other "gymnasts" in their gymnastics club or twirling around like the "ballerina" they imagine themselves to be, without looking at their bodies and thinking they need to change them.

I know coaches want to win. I know instructors want what is best for their students, and oftentimes what is best is gently pushing those students out of whatever lessons they're taking, because they're just not cut out for it. But using the body as a way to push them out? *That's not acceptable.*

I'm not saying that every coach is obsessed with winning. Not every coach would tell a little girl she is too fat or too tall or too slow or too whatever to succeed in her sport. Many coaches are loving, supportive mentors to our little girls, and that's a really amazing thing (thank you, supportive coaches). But until we can say that *all* of them are, we've got a problem on our hands.

I went through my high school, college, and young adult years starving myself, still trying to prove that I was thin enough to be beautiful, thin enough to be a successful journalist, thin enough to be a good dancer, thin enough to be graceful, thin enough to be accepted, and, sure, it wasn't all because of that ballet instructor, but the early memories of someone commenting negatively on a girl's body have a way of sinking down deep and festering there. So when we tell our six-year-old girls that they don't have a thin enough body to do (blank), what we're doing is handing them a ticket straight to eating disorder hell. Or body hatred hell. Or body dysmorphia hell. Or whatever it becomes in the life of that little girl. It manifests in many different ways. Anxiety, obsession, depression. Those, too.

Stop telling little girls they're not thin enough.

Stop exalting this ridiculous idea that there is only one body type that is beautiful. Stop ruining girls' perceptions of themselves. Stop making our little girls hyper-aware of their bodies before they're even able to properly spell the word "bodies."

I don't have a little girl. I don't get to assure her that she's beautiful just the way she was made. I don't get to tell her that she is perfect in every way. I don't get to explain that, yeah, it's good to make healthy choices and do good things for our bodies, but it's *never* okay to starve ourselves to fit a certain prototype that is applauded above all the others.

But I have nieces. And I will tell them every chance I get:

You are beautiful just the way you are.

You are more than your body. So much more.

Don't ever let someone tell you that you can't do something just because of the way you look. You are brave and creative and kind and strong and loved and good enough.

Because these are the things I wish someone had told me.

Gender Lines: a Short Examination

The other day I walked outside to call my boys in for dinner, and I found something extraordinary: four of them were playing with the little girl who lives next door to us. All her My Little Ponies and Barbies were scattered everywhere on the driveway, and my sons were making them talk, making her laugh, and making themselves laugh, too.

Some men might find this something close to offensive. I am married to a man who does not worry about four of his six sons playing with Barbies and My Little Ponies.

We just smiled at the picture of the four of them collaboratively imagining whole new worlds—without fighting (that's a miracle in and of itself)—and left them to play with the neighbor girl for a few extra minutes. Dinner could wait.

This gender issue can get a little messy.

Everywhere you go—stores, schools, libraries, museum gift shops—you don't have to look far to find gender separation. Girls are pink and purple and frilly and sparkly. Boys are blue and black and matte and dignified. Girls have superstars and bows. Boys have superheroes and cowboy hats.

The implied messages here are, "Boys wear this. Girls wear that. Boys play with this. Girls play with that."

When I was a kid, one of my favorite things to do was dig Hot Wheels paths out in the backyard dirt. My brother and I would play for hours, making parking garages and stores and neighborhoods and the roads that connected them all. I would build LEGO creations with him for days upon weeks. He would play Barbies with me, although his play typically involved a tornado that would rip apart my Barbie mansion.

The point is, the gender division didn't seem so obvious in my house when I was a kid.

Now I'm the mom of only boys. The gender division is very obvious to me today. Every time I take my kids into a department store, they can tell which aisles are made for them.

We had a birthday party yesterday, and my six-year-old got some superhero LEGO collections. The first thing he said, after all his friends left, was, "Will you put this together with me, Mama?"

"Mama doesn't like superhero LEGOs," my four-year-old said.

"Yes, she does," my six-year-old said.

"No. She likes princess ones," my four-year-old said. "She's a girl."

I beg to differ. I told them that my favorite LEGO sets are not the ones designated for girls; they're the Star Wars ones.

That afternoon, I sat down with both of them and put together Spider-Man's fight scene with Dr. Octopus like a *boss*.

I want my boys to know, despite what others may tell them, that playing across the gender lines is completely acceptable and even highly encouraged. I daily show my resistance by sword fighting with them, racing them on Mario Kart, and begging them to play dolls with me.

Who says the world has to be so pink and blue?

On Mental Health and Parenting: a Declaration

I talk about a whole lot of things when it comes to my parenting life. What I don't often mention, or even admit to those who know me, is the fact that I live with perpetual anxiety.

I'm not just talking about normal anxiety, either, worrying about your kids and the future for a fleeting moment in time. My worry is practically ever-present, always around, always waiting, always watching for the perfect moment to knock my feet out from under me—or, more accurately, knock the breath from my chest. This kind of anxiety carries me away on a riptide of negativity so strong that I can't swim against it no matter how many pushups I've done to strengthen my upper body.

Children, of course, haven't made my anxiety any easier. In fact, they've made it more challenging in some ways. Not only do I worry about my job and our finances and the state of my health, but I worry about their school careers and their friend choices and whether or not their health is what it should be.

I don't always know when my anxiety attacks will hit me.

Sometimes an attack blindsides me because the oldest got in trouble at school, and I can't help but think that the same old behaviors are going to show themselves and we'll be right back where we started four years ago, before we learned how to better handle a strong-willed, sometimes depressed kid. Sometimes an attack sneaks up on me because someone got hurt or is sick and I wonder if this is worse than everybody thinks it is and whether or not I'll be asked to say goodbye to one of my sons. Sometimes one chases me because one of my sons walked himself to school and I can only imagine all the bad things that must have happened on the way and now I regret not being a parent who gives her elementary school kids a cell phone.

This anxiety has tailed me since I was a kid. If my mom was more than a minute late to pick me up from any pre-arranged pickup spot, I imagined all sorts of ways she must have died, followed by all the things I would do to make sure my brother and sister and I were taken care of.

In the last several weeks, I have lived in the dark, cold cavern of nearly debilitating anxiety. About three months ago, at the start of the summer, I was reading to my boys from one of the chapter books we'd chosen, and a blind spot suddenly showed up in my right eye. It was a neat and tidy little gray square that put me into a quick and efficient panic attack while the open book shook in my hands. I felt the warm rush and the rock at the back of my throat, and I tried to hold it together while I finished up reading and then called Husband, because I was sure that my retina was tearing loose from my eye.

Husband rushed home, took over with the boys, and I sped down the road to my eye doctor.

There was no retinal tear. There was no floater, even, that the magnification could detect. There was nothing. "Are you a Type A personality?" my doctor said. I laughed a little and told her about some of my weird little things. I told her that I'm a mom of six boys. "All right then," she said. "It's most likely an ocular migraine that will go away."

I asked her if I should wear an eye patch in the meantime, since I'd just secured one for the seven-year-old's Halloween costume, and I knew my boys would get a kick out of a mama pirate, but she said no, it should go away with time. So I just wore the cool roll-up sunglasses they give you for eye dilation and listened to my boys laugh themselves silly when I walked in the door at home.

Fast forward three months. The spot did not go away.

So, after dealing with a week of intense anxiety—I was losing my sight, I would be blind forever, or maybe I had MS or maybe there was a brain tumor or what if it got worse and what would my boys do without me—I went to see my primary care doctor. Anxiety made it hard to breathe in his office. I was afraid I would not get to watch my boys grow up. I was afraid I would not be able to watch anything at all. I was afraid that all the rough drafts of stories on my computer hard drive would never be finished.

But I pulled it together, because I'm a mother and I'm good at that sort of thing, and I acted like everything was just fine. I cried in the car on the way home.

The doctor ordered an MRI, and I worried for a week about what that MRI might find. I could hardly breathe in my house. I could not think about what was for dinner or what to do about the kid who was pounding his brother or what to say to Husband, who watched helplessly while I obsessed over a small gray square. I could not paddle out of the cavern, no matter how hard I tried. We celebrated our anniversary. I thought only of the impending MRI.

The MRI showed a perfectly normal brain, though we all know that "perfectly normal" is relative. I know, from this experience, that my brain is not, in fact, perfectly normal. I tried to tell myself it was for a while, because this isn't something that's generally accepted by the wider public. Mental health is a shaky issue. The people who struggle with it are people who are not *normal,* who are not *right,* who are not *acceptable.*

Forget that.

I've hidden my anxiety for a long time. Those of us who live with mental health issues tend to hide them—because we think, deep down, that maybe something is wrong with us, that maybe we *aren't* normal or right or acceptable. We try to pretend we're okay. We try to put on a brave face for the world, even though we can feel the dark cloud shaking over us. We try to ignore it for as long as we possibly can.

I woke my boys up for school and cooked their breakfast and helped them pack up and listened to the six of them talk to me all at the same time and dropped the school ones off at their elementary and prepared lunch and read stories and did my five hours of work every day and sat through loud dinners and oversaw their baths and read stories again and helped them brush their teeth and put them to bed and put them to bed again, and I tried my best to outrun this defect. This monster. This unacceptable proof of my weakness.

But here's the thing: because of my anxiety, because of my brain's ability to take a normal situation and twist it into something to be feared and dreaded, I will likely have one or more children who struggle with the same disorder. So if I hide, what do they learn? They learn that they, too, must hide. And the only thing hiding does is isolate.

These last few weeks, when anxiety has gnawed away at my heart and my mind and my emotions, I have withdrawn from everyone and everything. I do my work, because my work sustains me. But I could not formulate thoughts to Husband. I could not bear the loud voices of my children. I could not look my friends in the eye, because I knew that as soon as they asked me how I was, I would crumble.

I don't want my boys to isolate themselves. Isolation is one of the leading causes of suicide. There are one hundred seventeen suicides committed every single day in our world. White males account for seven out of ten of those. That's a scary statistic for the mother of six white males.

No more.

No more hiding. No more shame. No more pretending that I can handle anything and everything.

Mental health is a really big deal. The number of children in our world today who have some kind of mental health issue is staggering. I want my boys and all children to know and understand the value of sharing about our struggles. I want them to know that we do not have to hide. I want them to know the value of talking about mental health issues and seeking help when we cannot manage our disorders ourselves. I want them to understand that when they are swept into the cavern, they do not go alone.

We go together. And we fight our way, paddle by paddle, back out.

How to Drive in a Neighborhood With Children: Carefully

There is one thing I hate above all the others. Actually, there are many, but admitting that doesn't serve the purpose of this essay. So the one thing I hate above the others is this: driving recklessly through a neighborhood where children are walking or playing.

There are several definitions of driving recklessly—at least according to me. There is speeding, there is breaking traffic laws, there is texting or doing anything at all with a phone while your hands are on the wheel.

I am fortunate enough to live right down the road from my boys' elementary school. Every morning, we wake up, do the morning rush, and race out the door to walk the four blocks and hopefully arrive at the doors before the tardy bell rings.

It seems many other people in my neighborhood are in a hurry, too—especially the ones who drive.

It must be said: There is nothing—no amount of lateness in the world, no consequence for that lateness drastic enough—that is more important than the safety of a child.

One recent morning, when my sons and I were walking to school, we almost lost a kid. The three-year-old twins were running ahead, and though I've told them a billion times not to cross the street in front of me, when I arrived at the crosswalk, one of them took my mere presence as permission to cross. He took off running, thinking I would be right there with him. I screamed his name in the feral way all mothers scream their kid's name when there is danger present. I could see that the young woman who was approaching the stop sign was not paying attention but was, instead, looking down at something—I could later tell, in a flash of a moment, that the something was her phone. She did not consider it imperative to stop at the stop sign.

Thankfully, at the last minute, my feral scream slammed into my son, turned him around, and shot him back to the sidewalk.

The young woman did not even see him as she rolled through the stop sign.

I could hardly breathe. And then I could hardly see; the fury was so thick and wild. I wished, maturely, that I had a collection of rotten eggs to toss at her car, to make her look up, to make her see what had almost happened in her hurry.

Instead, I knelt level with my little boy, who doesn't fully understand the dangers of running out into a street yet, and I told him, as I've told him many times, never, ever, ever to cross a street without Mama or Daddy or one of his older brothers. I hugged him tight and tried not to think about what might have happened if he hadn't, for once, turned around and run back to me. Would the woman have noticed the crunch under her tires? Would she have realized her error? Would her life have been over as mine would have been, too?

As I write these words, I shudder.

I have to say it again: There is nothing—no important meeting, no to-do list item, no text or social media comment or navigational map you must pull up—that is more important than the safety of a child.

The problem is, most of the time, we're on autopilot. We drive without thinking. We pick up our phones without thinking. We roll through stop signs without thinking.

We could hit children without thinking.

This is the danger that exists in neighborhoods like mine, where kids walk to school.

And in neighborhoods like this, we need to slow down, put our phones down, and look. The world is not going to end because you did.

Call me selfish, but I don't want the life of one of my children to end because someone thought checking their email was more important than checking a crosswalk. I don't want to lose a son who trips on his untied shoelace and accidentally steps off the sidewalk for a split second to someone who is late, has no time to observe the school zone speed limit, and is going too fast to stop. I'm tired of crossing residential streets, wondering if the person roaring up the hill even sees me and my entourage of kids.

That young woman? I doubt she learned her lesson. She didn't even see my little boy, didn't see us standing, waiting to cross the street, didn't acknowledge that she'd rolled right through the stop sign. She had no idea what her interesting phone and her reckless driving might have done. Maybe she won't know until the unthinkable happens.

I've often entertained fantasies about what I could do to slow people down in my neighborhood. Throw tacks under their tires as they pass. Rotten eggs launched at windows, maybe. Lob dirty, unsecured diapers at their trunk as they fly on by. But I'm not a litterer, and I'm not a cruel person, either.

In the meantime, I've become pretty good at memorizing license plates, compiling lists of offenses, and sending them in to the police department. I don't know if that will accomplish anything. Maybe they'll get a ticket in the mail. Maybe the policeman in charge of vetting email will roll his eyes and think, *Just another complaint from Ms. Toalson* and toss it in the virtual trash where it will join thousands or (more likely) no other complaints like it.

I watch my children, the roads, and other drivers with eagle eyes. I talk to my sons, who are years away from being drivers, about the importance of responsible driving and ensuring that lives aren't in danger because of their foolish choices. I hope, endlessly, for more responsible drivers and better safety precautions to protect my children—our children—in their childhoods.

And I make sure I'm leading the way.

The safety of our children is much more important than that text from a friend.

Put the phones down.

(If you get a random ticket in the mail, I apologize. But not really: stop driving recklessly in the neighborhood where my kids are walking. I'm taking numbers.)

Dear Kids: Here's What You Can Do Instead of Tech Time

Dear kids,

You recently declared that your daddy and I had much more to do when we were kids, and that, because of this and because of your lack of things to do in contemporary life, we should let you have "a ton of technology time." What else will you do with your time? you said.

I thought it would be helpful for me to make a list of activities you could do when you find yourself getting bored and wishing for more technology time that is not going to be granted. You can refer back to this list as often as you need it.

But first I feel it necessary to tell you that when I was a kid, there was no technology time. My family, for a while, didn't have a Nintendo gaming system; it was too expensive. We also didn't have a home computer in our house until I was a senior in high school; it, too, was too expensive.

Instead of technology time, I could often be found reading in a hammock out in our yard, playing pyramid with the girls down the street, and engaging in a dangerous game of Red Rover until someone got their windpipe bruised because we weren't letting go, no matter what, and the game was, forever afterward, banned. Then we started playing hide-and-seek in the dark, which was freaky out in the country where snakes and all kinds of scary things lived.

I would take walks, exploring the country; I would search for interesting bugs in ditches; I would, mostly, read. That's not so surprising.

You all think I have a problem with tech time. I don't really. You're allowed to have daily tech time from 3:30 to 4 p.m. as long as you're done with the long list of things we require you to do—which you say, every day, is "so unfair." But, to us, it's important that tech time is earned; you'll understand this, perhaps, someday when you have kids of your own.

In the space between waking and tech time and tech time and sleeping, here are some things you can do:

Write a story about all the reasons I had more to do as a kid than you do today. Keep in mind that we didn't have things like Pokémon cards and the massive collection of board games in our game closet. I pretty much had a pair of roller skates, a rocky road out front, a hammock in the side yard, some Barbies, a few books at my disposal, plenty of notebooks, and a bike. Your aunt and I used to ride the old gas tank like a horse. We would pretend we were knighted princesses gone to save a kingdom, and whoever made it to the horse first was the hero; the other would be lost in the battle.

Count the clouds. Or, better yet, imagine what's in the clouds. This was one of my favorite things to do as a kid. I would imagine beings in the clouds. I would make up stories about them. One day I'll tell you a few.

Dust the house. God knows there's enough dust to go around, even if all six of you carried around a feather duster. And, no, we won't pay you. You get room and board.

Tie a bungee cord around your waist, attach it to the brick mailbox, and see how far you can run-skate down the hill with one roller blade before it pulls you back.

Wrestle on the stairs, which I normally wouldn't recommend, but if you're looking for danger like what is found in Breath of the Wild, then there it is.

Play Power Rangers on the trampoline, which would make you feel like you're actually a legitimate Power Ranger.

Make a club that includes all the kids on the block. You could make it a running club or a trampoline jumping club or an Explore Nature club. As long as its members stayed outside.

Sell Minecraft ideas in a lemonade-looking stand. This might give you some extra spending money. At the very least, it would get you out of the house where I don't have to hear you complain about how much you wish you could have more tech time.

Organize the game closet. That should take you a couple of hours. And it would be fair, considering you're the one who messed it up, and you're nothing if not overzealous in your destruction.

Wipe down all the books in our house, which would take all day and then some.

Actually read those books. There's a novel thought (pun intended).

Count your teeth—or anything else.

Write an essay on why all the plants in our house are dying—I bet you'd have some interesting things to say about that, wouldn't you? I know it's not me killing them. They get watered at least every two weeks.

Wash all the cups you used in the last hour. I see about fifteen of them.

Go outside and try to dig to the earth's mantle. I bet you'd even find a treasure of some kind or another.

Make an obstacle course through the already-messed-up playroom. You probably wouldn't even be able to tell a difference from the way it normally looks.

Write a silly book or illustrate some coloring pages—Christmas will be here before you know it, and we're always looking for gift ideas.

Teach yourself to whistle. Lots and lots of fun there.

Practice tying your shoes. Several of you could really use that practice.

Try licking your elbow or measuring your hand against your face—but for the latter one, make sure you're standing near me.

Sleep.

Pick up after yourself.

Read, read, and read. I know I already said this plenty of times, but reading a book provides you with hours of entertainment. It's a gift to yourself.

There are plenty of things to do if you'll just look around and use those big, bright imaginations you have.

If those screens in front of your face haven't melted them entirely.

I love you (if you can believe it) more than you love your tech time.

Kisses and hugs,

Mama

Child Leashes Save Lives and Sanity

My family makes quite a spectacle when we go out in public. There are eight of us, but this isn't what drops the jaws of those around us. What drops their jaws is the fact that seven of us are male.

If or when you see us on the streets of my city, you will likely see someone lagging far behind and someone else racing far ahead. Since our twins grew out of traveling in a stroller, this has become even more pronounced. Which means, for safety measures, we had to invest in some backpack leashes.

You probably already know about this interesting invention, but I'll tell you my take anyway. The foundation of today's backpack leashes is a cute little stuffed animal—we have a bear and a monkey missing two ears because my twins are nothing if not destructive. These leashes have a harness you can strap to your toddler's body. The tail of whatever animal you've chosen has a leash you can hold so if your kid happens to run out into the parking lot like it's a fun game to get smashed by the tires of a car, you can steer him back from his overzealous play.

Hypothetically.

At first I felt bad about using these leashes. Before I was a parent, I'd seen other parents using them and always thought them cruel and distasteful (the leashes, not the parents).

So many things change when you have children, including your attitude about putting kids on a leash.

The first time one of my twins was released from the confines of our car and darted straight for the road while we were wrestling another kid away from the packed lunch and I, in my eighth month of pregnancy with his little brother, raced to save him from an unsuspecting driver barreling toward him, I just about had a heart attack (not to mention what happened to my pants). I didn't think I was going to make it. (That was nothing compared to the next day, though. I could hardly move, I was so sore.)

And I knew we had to do something about our toddlers' freedom. I knew I wasn't getting any faster, and they weren't getting any fewer. There were two of them, after all. One could distract both parents (it takes two to handle one of them) while the other did God knows what.

Leashes it was.

The first time we used our backpack leashes was on a family trip to the San Antonio Zoo. The leashes saved our twins' lives seventeen billion times—and that was before we even left the parking lot.

Say what you want to say about what that indicates—I'll probably agree. They're impulsive boys who don't think about the consequences of their actions. They don't hear us unless we raise our voices (and their hearing has always tested fine). They are the most difficult of our children to manage.

So we slap leashes on them.

Child leashes make other people uncomfortable. I get it; as I admitted above, I used to be uncomfortable with them, too. But after a certain point, don't you trust a parent to do what's best for their kids?

Seems lots of people actually don't. When Husband and I are walking past the local zoo's dining area, where our kids always loudly complain about how hungry they are, people make a point to catch our eye and then, while we're looking, shake their heads at our cruelty (maybe it's the kids complaining of hunger, not the leashes. We'll never know. I don't really care.). When we are speed-walking past the alligators (leashes only protect from so much), on our way to the petting zoo, people eye Husband and me like we're the Worst Parents Ever (we are, according to our still-hungry kids). When we're in the middle of a crowd because everyone's trying to see the panther that just woke up, and someone, who wasn't paying attention, runs right into the leash, that someone scowls at us.

Most of the time, I take it like a champ. People don't know others' reality until they live it.

Sometimes, though, I say things that are almost guaranteed to make those scowlers even more convinced of my awful parenting. Here are a few of those things.

1. "Oh, don't mind me. I'm just taking my kids for a walk."

I like to save this one for the dog owners we pass who actually leash their dogs. They look at me like I'm a disgusting excuse for a parent, but do I care? The answer to that question is no.

2. "Kids are like dogs—may as well leash them."

I'm only speaking the truth. You throw a ball to a toddler, and he will happily retrieve it for you, maybe even with his tongue out. A toddler will pee wherever he wants to, as if he's marking his territory. You chase a kid, and he will hightail it out of there, just like any spooked dog. And if you've ever been kissed by an eighteen-month-old with bad aim, you know it's exactly like a face full of dog slobber (except much sweeter, in my opinion).

3. "You should see them when they're not leashed."

This is all in good fun, but seriously. You do not want to see our twins unleashed. It is physically impossible for them to stay in one place. The times we've been brave enough to let them walk without holding onto the bear's or monkey's tail, we always regret that small taste of freedom.

Also, unleashed, my twins would very likely do something ridiculously stupid. They have no concept of what is dangerous and what is not, and I wouldn't put it past them to nip at the heels of the cars speeding by. Pardon me if I don't want them flattened beneath the tires of someone (a) going way too fast, (b) playing with their cell phone, or (c) likely both.

4. "It's a good thing they invented kid leashes, huh? Keeps them in one place for however long you want. I use them all the time in my backyard!"

I like to say this to make scowlers think that we actually use our kid-leashes for other times besides when we're walking in the middle of a crowded, dangerous place. (We don't.) You should see their faces.

5. "If you loved them, then you shoulda put a leash on them."

This is usually sung facetiously to the tune of Beyonce's hit song, "Single Ladies." It's great when you're going for surprise that quickly turns into judgment. My favorite.

6. "Oh, okay. I'll let out the slack a little. They like knowing they have a little freedom, right? But not too much. Can't be too careful."

I punctuate this with a crazy little cackle, because, well, I like them to look at me like I'm crazy. Because I kind of am. And it's funny, because backpack leashes don't actually have slack. They're made so that a kid can only be a few feet away from you, which is where they're safest.

We've slowly ~~trained~~ helped our twins to better accept the reality of their leashes, and they no longer pull against them. In fact, they take their captivity like champs. And every now and then, we'll feel a bit hopeful and try the whole freedom thing again. We'll tuck their leash-tails into the backpack part and point out the elusive panther as we pass. It takes them only moments to do exactly what we expect them to do: divide and conquer, except it's not so much conquering as it is disappearing so completely that we'll spend the next half hour trying to locate them, hoping they're not the kid on the evening news who was mauled by a tiger.

Husband will enlist the help of several zoo employees while I stay put trying not to lose any more children. And just when we're about to lose hope, our missing son will come careening toward us, running for his life, because there's a zoo employee trying to pick him up, and he doesn't talk to strangers.

The leashes will not come off for the rest of the day, and our son won't even whine or yip about it.

Hypothetically.

Say what you want to say. I know those leashes save lives.

The Energetic, Enigmatic Nature of Boy Play

Husband and I recently received a communication from our son's fourth-grade teacher. Recess, the email said, was temporarily suspended for some problems kids were having on the playground.

They have since rescinded their punishment of the kids and found an alternative to it, but the possibility of these no-recess days got me thinking about the expectations we hold for young children—especially boys—in our schools.

Because I'm a mom of six boys, I get to see many different personalities slide out in the course of boy play. And even while one will choose to build quietly with wooden planks for his free play time and another will reach for a book and another still will race out to the backyard shrieking like a banshee and thrusting his pirate sword into the belly of an imaginary enemy, there are some things that come pretty standard in boy play.

1. They run.

On our walk to school, my sons can't simply walk. They can't. They run the entire way. I always say this is why I wear workout clothes most days—I have to keep up with my sons somehow. This is only halfway true…the other half of the truth is that I didn't get a shower today, and, also, it's a thousand degrees in Texas; may as well sweat in actual workout clothes. It somehow makes it better.

My standard footwear is my cross training shoes, because there is absolutely no telling when I will have to break out into a sprint to save a boy from a mistimed run or a fall that happened when they were engaged in a race with themselves.

2. They shriek.

No matter what boys are doing, they're loud. If they're sweeping the kitchen floor, they're singing "Thriller" at the top of their lungs. If they're running through the backyard playing Infected (a variation on chase, as far as we can tell, where the person who's "It" adds an army of people who are "It"), they're shrieking at the top of their lungs.

Incidentally, when we asked what happened on the school playground, my fourth grader said, "I don't really know. I think a couple of boys got into a fight, but I was playing Infected, so I was running for my life."

3. They fight.

For fun, my boys play a fight game. They call it "Slap Fight From Noon 'Til Night." Sometimes there are variations on this fight game. Sometimes they use a superhero cape to whip the legs out from under their opponent and end up with welts on their shins. Sometimes they take plastic swords out to the trampoline and whack each other with ill-aimed blows. Sometimes they just use their hands.

This is all for fun. It's as delightful as it sounds.

4. They bounce.

Boys are bundles of energy, and if Husband and I are doling out instructions, saying something serious, or just mushily telling them we love them so so much, my sons are forever and always bouncing. They bounce on their bottoms, they bounce on their bellies, they bounce on their knees. They bounce so much it makes me sore watching them.

5. They very rarely think before doing.

The most frequent answer to "What were you thinking" after a kid has busted his face on the side of our brick house, at which he ran full speed ahead to test his stopping reflexes, is "I don't know." And it's true. They don't know.

When my sons do stupid things like try to jump from the trampoline to the top of their dad's shed fourteen feet away, act on their insatiable curiosity about what it's like to pee off the top of our van, or ride down the stairs on a skateboard, I already know the answer to my deepest wondering.

6. They compete.

Whatever boys are doing, it's a fierce competition. They will simultaneously swing across the monkey bars to see who can finish first, knocking out teeth in the process. They will race to the end of the sidewalk to see who wins on the way to check the mail. They will eat their food—practically inhale it—so they can be the first one done and in line for seconds (there is no line. We don't even dole out seconds until everyone has finished their firsts. Does it matter? Nope.).

7. They lose all sense of time and space.

When they're little, boys don't have much of a sense of their body, which is why they'll barrel into their mother, nearly knocking her flat, when they decide they want to give her a hug. They also have no sense of time. "I'll be done in two minutes," they say, and what they really mean is twenty.

(This doesn't change as they get older, unfortunately. Husband will often say, "I'm almost done," and two hours later he's finally ready for our date night at home. I'm already asleep.)

8. They're gross.

They compare the boogers they picked from their noses, they collectively gather in the bathroom to see poop before it's flushed, they like nothing more than to announce to the house and the entire world, "He's bleeding!"

On a regular basis, my boys try to determine who has the smelliest farts. They will sulfurize each other out of a room before they declare a winner—and by then no one's conscious to celebrate.

Girls have their challenges in a society like ours; I struggle with those challenges every day.

Boys have their challenges, too, and they can be seen, most often, in the early classrooms of their childhood. It's unfortunate that all across the nation, boys are monthly, weekly, daily punished for who they are. Of course they must learn how to take control of their bodies and navigate a social world that needs softer voices and better attention—but never at the cost of their identity.

My boys drive me perpetually crazy, but I know that one

day I'll miss being jostled on my way to the bathroom, knocked sideways into a stream of crop-dust because they wanted to get there first.

Boys will be boys. And I love them for it.

Don't miss out on a Crash Test Parents release!
Visit www.racheltoalson.com to keep up-to-date on book and product releases and to access bonus material.

Appendix A: 11 Reasons I'm the Worst Mom Ever

#035:
I make my kids do chores.

#036:
I won't let them have five cookies.

#037:
I won't let them pummel each other until one begs mercy.

#038:
I make them clean up after themselves.

#039:
I won't let them run out in front of a car.

#040:
I expect them to conduct themselves like decent human beings before I let them have tech time.

#041:

I said it's bedtime.

#042:

I told him there's no purple plate when he asked if he could have the purple plate.

#043:

I won't let them watch three hundred hours of television.

#044:

I won't let them eat their weight in pre-Thanksgiving pumpkin pie.

#045:

I make them take baths.

Appendix B: 19 Real-Life Conversations with Kids

Husband: What do you want for a snack?
5-year-old: Peanut butter and...season salt!

7-year-old: Today I dared my friend to step in an ant pile. And he dared me. And we both did it.
Husband: That's definitely not a dare you should do.
7-year-old: Why not?

Me: Are you even listening to me?
9-year-old: Okay, I wasn't listening. But do I at least get credit for telling you I wasn't listening?

Meghan Trainor: My name is no, my sign is no, my number is no...
7-year-old: I don't like this song. It teaches boys to give up.

Me: Stay down here with me. I'm afraid.
5-year-old: What are you afraid of?
Me: My imagination.

5-year-old: I'm afraid of the clowns that kill people.

Me: Can a woman do anything as well as a man can?
9-year-old: Well, not everything. Take armpit farts, for example.

Me: What's going on out there?
Husband: Ah. Hoosies.
Me: What?
Husband: Exactly.
[Kid's voice leaking through the door: I don't want any Hoosies!]

Me: Come on, hurry up. We have to go pick up your brothers.
4-year-old: What does hurry mean?
Me:
4-year-old:
Me:
4-year-old: What?

7-year-old: It reminds me of the NFL—you know, the National Football...Liver."
Me: Yeah, we're not sports people, are we.

3-year-old: WHY DID YOU TAKE AWAY MY NAPKIN?
Me: Because you were tearing it up.
3 year-old: NO! I was making something and then

breaking it!!

> 7-year-old: Oh, I put some butt cheek prints on the mirror.
> Me: Why would you do that?
> 7-year-old: Because it's funny.

> 9-year-old: My horoscope says live tonight like there's no tomorrow. So I guess I'll just panic.

> 7-year-old: I drew an emoji on my paper today to express how I was feeling. It was a happy face.
> Me: In my day we called that a happy face.
> 7-year-old:
> Me:
> 7-year-old: Well, you're old.

> Husband: [rolling down the window] Oh my gosh, who did that?
> 9-year-old: hahahahahah
> Me: So gross.
> 9-year-old: Daddy, you're going to make all our Pokémon cards fly away!
> Me: Well, you should have thought about that before you let your cheeks flap.

> 7-year-old: [walking around the store taking every sample he can find] What I like about samples is that they're free.

9-year-old: In my lifetime, I've let out thousands of farts.
Me:
9-year-old: That's probably hundreds of victims.
Me:
9-year-old: I'm just guessing.

Me: Every time I try to take a sip of my smoothie, I get a big whiff of fart.
Boys: hahahahahahahaha

9-year-old: If I liked a girl, I would create a robot to go ask her if she likes anyone.
Husband: And then what?
9-year-old: And if she mentioned me, the robot would tell me.
Husband: And then what?
9-year-old: And I would tell her about the robot and she would like me more.
Husband: And then what?
9-year-old: I don't know.
Me: Maybe you could invite her over for dinner.
9-year-old: Ummm…probably not.
Me:
Husband:
[Everyone looking at the table, where boys are arm farting their ABCs]
Me: Yeah. That's probably a good decision.

Husband: What do you think would happen if we let you eat anything you wanted all the time?

7-year-old: We would be happy.

About the Author

Rachel is the CBS (Chief Battle Strategist) in the Toalson home, scanning hills, ignoring the ones that don't matter, and braving the ones that do. Today she has let one of her sons out of the house with soccer socks that came up to his thighs (because they're not his; he just wanted to wear them), shorts that belonged to his two-years-younger brother (everybody's talking 'bout his tight pants), and flip flops. It's an unimportant hill, this one of style. What she didn't let her son do was rot his brain on technology all day, like he wanted to do—because this is a hill that matters to her.

When she's not strategizing about which battles to engage and which battles to quietly (or not so quietly) let slip by, Rachel writes essays, poetry, and fiction for children, teens, and adults. Sometimes it's funny.

Rachel lives with her husband and six sons in San Antonio, Texas, where she writes daily with headphones, holed up in her home-office bedroom. The kids still interrupt.

www.rachetoalson.com

Author's Note

My dear reader,

I hope that within the pages of this book, you have discovered your own battles that are worth fighting. I hope that you have given yourself permission to let go of those battles that don't matter as much, since no parent can fight every single battle our kids bring to us and slam at our feet, a challenge gleaming in their eyes. I hope you have laughed in recognition at the inconceivable inconsistencies of both your children and yourself. We are all masters of paradox and contradiction. It is called being human.

The essays within this book, as I'm sure you have noticed, are not written as prescriptive commentaries on how to parent. They are written to entertain, to encourage, to turn a heart toward laughter, which I believe turns a heart more securely toward joy. Parenting may be hard, but at least there is laughter to soften the blows and falls.

Thank you, as always, for supporting my work. Please consider leaving a review wherever you bought it. Reviews do a number of things; most importantly, they help get books into the hands of other readers.

And if you can think of anyone who needs a little laughter

in his or her parenting life, please share this book with them. There is nothing more bolstering than recognizing that you and your kids are not so different from other parents and other kids.

Fight strong and smart.

In love,

Rachel

Acknowledgments

A book is a joint enterprise—from conception to completion. So thank you to:

My children: You never cease to amaze me and inspire me and practically write my humor pieces for me. I love you, I adore you, I'm thankful for you, and please forgive me for telling all our secrets.

Ben: Your support is practically otherworldly; thank you for telling me when I'm being snarky, for sometimes laughing out loud (it's always my goal), and for not thinking I'm crazy when you walk in and I'm reading out loud to myself. Or maybe you think I'm crazy, in which case—don't tell me.

My mom: Thanks for always encouraging my sense of humor.

My mom friends: Isn't it great to know we're not alone?

My readers: I'm always glad you came around.

Thank you, all, for your loyalty, your encouragement, and your very large presence in my life.

Crash Test Parents

Enjoy more from the Crash Test Parents series:

www.crashtestparents.com

Are you a parent who needs a little dose of humor and hope?

For a limited time, pick up your FREE copies of *Guide to Surviving a Year* and *Guide to Self Esteem* and laugh your way back into hope. Or maybe just survival.

Get your FREE copies at:
racheltoalson.com/SurvivingAYear

www.ingramcontent.com/pod-product-compliance
Lightning Source LLC
Chambersburg PA
CBHW021428080526
44588CB00009B/463